MAKING A DIFFERENCE IN YOUR WORLD

To Sandra,
You
make the
difference!
Love,
Bobbie Sims

MAKING A DIFFERENCE IN YOUR WORLD

BOBBI SIMS

PELICAN PUBLISHING COMPANY
GRETNA 1985

First printing, May 1984
Second printing, October 1985

Library of Congress Cataloging in Publication Data
Sims, Bobbi.
  Making a difference in your world.
  1. Meditations. 2. Sims, Bobbi. I. Title.
BV4832.2.S527 1983 248.3'4 83-12162
ISBN 0-88289-420-X

Unless otherwise noted, Scriptures used are from the Revised Standard Version.
JBP indicates J. B. Phillips Translation; KJV indicates King James Version.
TEV indicates Today's English Version.

Manufactured in the United States of America
Published by Pelican Publishing Company, Inc.
1101 Monroe Street, Gretna, Louisiana 70053

CONTENTS

ACKNOWLEDGMENTS 7
PROLOGUE 8
LESSONS FROM NATURE 9
IDENTITY 17
SELF-ESTEEM 27
LIVING IN THE NOW 33
MIND AND ATTITUDES 39
SELF-UNDERSTANDING 55
FEELINGS 63
RELATIONSHIPS 75
COMMUNICATION 85
RESPONSIBILITY 91
EVERYDAY LIVING 95
GOALS 105
LOVE 113
GOD 117
EPILOGUE 127

Dedicated to the people who lived these experiences. You have made a tremendous difference in my life. Thank you for being my living mirrors.

ACKNOWLEDGMENTS

There are two ways of spreading
light; to be the candle or the
mirror that reflects it.
Edith Wharton

Thinking about the experiences I might include in this book has created a tremendous amount of gratitude to all the people who have made a difference in my life and contributed to my growth. You have my love and thanks.

To Nina, who inspired me to add quotations and Scriptures to each story, and who served as my mentor as I worked through some of my personal blocks. To Sister Annette, who provided some of the quotations and Scriptures. To Ethel and Annette for providing perfect environments for writing. To Jim and Joy for proofreading and encouragement. To Charlotte for the initial editing. To Ruth, who suggested to Helen Kempe that she read my manuscript, and to Helen, who recommended the manuscript to Pelican Publishing Company. You two are very special ladies. To Gladys and Sheila, who typed with loving enthusiasm and accuracy. To the many other personal-growth educators who have provided me with excellent training and opportunities for my own development.

Finally, to my husband Larry, without whose love, support, and knowledge of writing this book would not have come about.

I gratefully acknowledge your contributions to my life and to this book.

PROLOGUE

Tis the good reader that makes a good
book . . . the profoundest thought or
passion sleeps as in a mine until it
is discovered by an equal mind and heart.
                    Ralph Waldo Emerson

I began to write this book after receiving much encouragement from members of the audiences at my speaking engagements. They suggested I put into writing the ideas I use in my talks. I got goose bumps every time the suggestion came up. Goose bumps are affirmations for me, so I began to let the idea take root. There was only one problem: I wasn't a writer. I did not even write letters to my family; when I want to communicate with them long distance, I telephone.

The message I had consistently been giving myself was, "I hate writing." One day I heard myself repeat that message and felt my gut tighten with hate. The full realization hit me that I had been using my good energy hating something as neutral as writing. I don't know when I decided to hate writing. When wasn't important. Since I had decided to hate writing, I could also decide to enjoy it. On that day I made a commitment to use my energy constructively and to learn to enjoy writing.

Being a "writer" is not a major goal of mine. What *is* important is that through the process of writing I have been able to share these experiences with you. It has been an exhilarating experience that has taught me a lot about me (not the least of which is to pay more attention to what I "hate," to examine it, and to rethink it).

I have used lofty quotations throughout the book. The lofty ideals are just that — lofty ideals — until they are turned into experiences. Should you see yourself in any of these mirrors and derive some benefit from them, that will be a bonus to add to my joy.

At the beginning God
expressed Himself.
John 1:1 (JBP)

8

LESSONS FROM NATURE

Nature and books belong to the eyes that see them.
Ralph Waldo Emerson

Yes, God gave us a rose garden
and we are unhappy because it is
full of thorns.

For much of my life I have had an attitude of "Yes, but": "Yes, it would be exciting to be a writer, but I am an ordinary person"; "Yes, but it shouldn't be that way"; "Yes, you are right, but . . . "

Finally I heard myself negating the "yeses" in my life with the "buts." I was spending so much energy complaining about the "buts" that I was not acknowledging and enjoying the "yeses."

Now every time I hear myself say, "Yes, but," I am aware that I may be resisting accepting what is.

All beliefs that I may have about what should be will not make any difference to what is. Changing the *but* to *and* allows me to accept what is. That acceptance brings me peace of mind and happiness.

Yes, I am an ordinary person, *and* I am doing extraordinary things with my life. Yes, you are right, *and* I don't want to agree with you. Yes, it shouldn't be that way, *and* that is the way it is.

Now I see life as a rose garden. It has its beauty, its color, its fragrance — *and* it is also full of thorns. Accepting the thorns as part of the garden has released me to enjoy the flowers.

Yes, life is beautiful, *and* it has its thorns.

Let us celebrate!
Luke 15:6 (TEV)

By virtue of being born to humanity, every human being has a right to the development and fulfillment of his potentialities as a human being.

Ashley Montagu

Contemplating the potential in us all, I remembered the giant pecan trees along the creek banks in Central Texas where I grew up, how they sprouted and grew without any help from anyone.

Those magnificent trees have always fascinated me. They fascinate me even more when I stop to think how each one started out as a small pecan. One little nut has the potential to become a giant tree that provides us with shade and food. I don't understand the mystery of how that happens, yet I have lived long enough and seen it happen often enough to know that it is so.

If the pecan is to become a giant tree it cannot be eaten; instead it becomes a seed. This seed has to come out of its shell in order to grow into a tree. As it grows toward maturity, the tree must face droughts, storms, and other natural perils. Each time the tree survives adversity it gains in strength and stature. It takes many years for the tree to reach its full maturity and bear pecans.

So it is with us. We too have to come out of our shells and risk adversity to grow toward our potential. We humans have at least as much potential as a nut! We don't have to understand this potential to use it. To start releasing our potential, we only need to acknowledge it.

Are you acknowledging and using your potential?

Every good endowment and every perfect gift is from above, coming from the Father of lights.
James 1:17

But what is happiness except
the simple harmony between a
man and the life he leads?
                            Albert Camus

The Frio River in South Central Texas is a magnificent, beautiful, crystal-clear river. Riding its rapids on an inner tube is one of my favorite forms of recreation.

The first time I rode the rapids I experienced both fear and delight. The fear was almost as strong as the delight. As I went through those very strong rapids I had no control—I went where the rapids took me. The fear and tension came from wanting to be in control. As I began to let go, stopped trying to stay in control, and learned a few ways that I could protect myself, there was less fear and more delight. Once I turned loose of my need to control, the river could provide me with both recreation and relaxation.

After becoming aware of my need to control the river I began to observe how often I wanted to stay in control of my life. Every time the need to control was present, so were fear and tension. Just as I can't control the river, I really don't have the power to control many of the situations I encounter or the actions of other people. When I shift my attention from controlling to guiding myself through situations and relationships, the tension and fear disappear.

When I don't attempt to control it, life becomes more pleasurable. Are you attempting to control your life, or moving in harmony with it?

Be not frightened, neither be
dismayed, for the Lord your
God is with you wherever you go.
                            Joshua 1:9

*Adversity introduces a person
to himself.*

Epictetus

For me, a good tonic is working in flower beds. It seems to clarify my mind and soul. Once, as I laboriously worked to get out the roots of the Bermuda grass that had invaded my flower beds, I became aware of how hard I was striving to get out every tiny little root. Then I remembered my Granddad, who was probably the greatest influence in my life, and how he would come by where we were working on the farm and say, "Get all those roots or the weeds will be right back." I smiled to myself as I thought of that lesson, and felt satisfied as I continued digging to "get all those roots." I began to reflect upon the lesson to see if it applied to the problems of life as well as to weeds.

In my dealings with people, all too often I observe them hard at work attempting to cure the symptoms of their problems rather than getting at the root causes. How easy it is to take a tranquilizer to alleviate a symptom rather than dig for the cause. Reflecting on my own life, I realized how a problem or unhappy situation has kept reappearing when I have only dealt with it on the surface.

Thank you, Granddad, for teaching me to go for the roots—of weeds, of difficulties in personal relationships, of communication breakdowns, or of any of life's other problems.

*To whom hath the root of
wisdom been revealed?
Ecclesiasticus 1:2
The Apocrypha*

You are the bows from which
your children as living
arrows are set forth.
Kahlil Gibran

While I was conducting a class for a group of teen-agers, three of them asked me to talk with their mothers about their over-protectiveness. I could understand the teens' point of view, and pondered about how I could get it across to their mothers.

Standing before a class of the mothers, I announced that some of their children had asked me to deliver a message. "I have decided to do this," I said, "by telling you a story.

"The story is about a beginning gardener. This gardener found rich, fertile soil under a large oak tree. He had it tested and cultivated. It was perfect soil. When he purchased some plants from a nursery, he got very specific instructions on how to plant them. He was very careful to follow these instructions and to water the plants regularly.

"Time passed. Still the garden didn't grow. The gardener went back to the nursery to find out what was wrong.

"The nurseryman asked him a number of questions, but was unable to determine the problem. Finally, he asked where the garden was located. The gardener replied, 'Under the protective shade of a big oak tree.'

" 'That is your problem,' the nurseryman explained. 'Gardens don't grow in the shade of trees.'

"Mothers, your children will not grow well in your shadows."

Let the children come to me, and
do not hinder them; for to such
belongs the kingdom of heaven.
Matthew 19:14

There is only one corner of the universe
you can be certain of improving, and
that's your own self.

Aldous Huxley

Tomatoes were selling for ninety-eight cents a pound in the grocery store. Growing in my backyard were tomatoes on the verge of ripening. There is nothing quite like growing your own, especially when they are so expensive in the store.

I did everything I could think of to hasten the growing process. The plants didn't ripen any faster. As I began to study my tomatoes I realized that ripening and maturing were the same process: when the tomato ripened it was mature. I could be helpful by supplying water and fertilizer; the tomato had to mature by itself.

Suddenly it occurred to me that people were the same way. Each person has to do his own maturing. We can give each other support, yet each of us is responsible for his own growth. As a wife, mother, and human-growth educator it was a relief to me to realize where my responsibility ended.

As I continued to study my garden I noticed that some of the tomatoes were like tiny hard green knots—they did not look as good as the ones on the verge of ripeness. When I looked at the more desirable tomato, I realized that it, too, had once been a tiny, hard, green knot. It had gone through different stages of growth, and each stage had been necessary. People, too, are in different stages of growth. Some stages appear more appealing than others, yet all stages are necessary steps to maturity, and each stage can be seen as part of the maturing process.

As I worked the bed where the tomatoes were growing, I saw the other fruits and vegetables I had planted. Each was very different from the others; the tomato was not like anything else growing in the bed. I realized that it is also a fact that I cannot be like anyone else. My sons can only be themselves, not the way I want them to be. There is as large a variety of people as there is a variety of fruits, vegetables, and flowers. As delicious as I find tomatoes, many people don't like them. So it is with people. Not everyone is going to like me—or you—as wonderful as we may be.

I turned back to the tomatoes, wondering what else they had to say to me. As I studied them this time I became conscious of the fact that each tomato was dependent for its growth on the vine itself, and on the soil, the sun, and the rain. I remembered my own struggle to be independent, how I went through a stage of thinking I did not need anyone. How wrong I was! There are many things I am unable to do for myself—like take out my own appendix, build my own house, or repair my own car. Each person has a talent and we are all dependent on one another. As I thought about the tomato drawing sustenance from the vine, I decided that if I was going to believe that I was created of God I too might draw from Him the nutrients that I need to grow and mature.

It also occurred to me that the tomato would mature as long as it was attached to the vine. It had no power to prevent its own growth. Only in the human form do we differ; as people, we can prevent our maturing. We don't mature when we are stuck in an old pattern of thinking and behaving. We can grow toward maturity only when we are willing to open our eyes and look for constructive ways to think and behave.

I have not only enjoyed raising and eating tomatoes, I have also enjoyed what they have taught me about myself and other people.

I am the true vine and my
Father is the vine dresser.
John 15:1

IDENTITY

*A sense of identity is so vital
that a person ultimately must
find some means of satisfying it.*
Erich Fromm

If God is thy father,
man is thy brother.
  Lamartine

When I was a child, people often told me I looked like my mother, and that comparison made me furious. As we both have gotten considerably older and I see how well my mother has held up, that comparison gives me hope.

For the last few years I've been looking at physical characteristics and genetic strengths and weaknesses that I have inherited from my parents. I have become conscious of attitudes and behavior patterns I learned from them. *Yes,* I have inherited much from my parents, *and* I am not limited to that inheritance or that identity.

As I began to extend my identity beyond that of my parents, I started to see both my parents and myself as God's children. I began seeing us as equals. I could then focus on our being God's children and what that means. The limits of who I am were immediately expanded. If we have inherited genetic characteristics from our earthly parents, I thought, maybe we have some kind of similar inheritance from the Creator of this universe. I don't think God is freckled and redheaded, as I am, so what may I have inherited from Him?

As I contemplate His nature, I see Him as love and energy — as creative, as knowing, as emotional, as purposeful. Could His nature also be our nature? Choosing to believe that we are created in His image and have inherited His nature has motivated me to change my identity to "God's child" and to work to accept my inheritance.

Who are you identifying with, and how is it affecting you?

> *Whereby are given unto us exceeding*
> *great and precious promises: that*
> *by these ye might be partakers of the*
> *divine nature.*
> *2 Peter 1:4 (KJV)*

To be nobody but yourself in a
world which is doing its best night
and day to make you everybody else,
means to fight the hardest battle
which any human being can fight and
never stop fighting.

e e cummings

An expression one frequently hears is, "I've got to go out and find myself." A friend told me about an acquaintance of hers whose husband asked for a divorce, saying he had to go out and find himself. He did, in fact, go out and find a new wife; I don't know if he ever found himself.

Men and women quit jobs and leave their families in their search for themselves. Young people leave home or school with the explanation, "I've got to go find myself." Every time I hear that expression my first thought is always, "Where are you going to look for yourself?" It's as though one's self is *out there* somewhere. It's this "out there" that I feel so puzzled about. How can you *be* in one place and have to look for yourself in another?

I wonder if what these people are really saying is, "I feel I can't be myself in this environment, so I'm going where I can." I also suspect that they will not give themselves permission to be as they want to be, so they look for someone else to give them that permission.

I have discovered that I can find myself only within myself, *where* I am, right now. Where are you looking?

... for I am fearfully
and wonderfully made.
Psalms 139:14 (KJV)

20

*I am not only the actor, but
the director of the acting.*
                Roberto Assagioli

One of the most frequent goals my students speak of is gaining a sense of identity. Being told who we are is not meaningful; identity can only be experienced, and it is only from the experience that real meaning is derived.

Psychologist J. F. T. Bugental defines a sense of identity as "the sense of 'being there' in one's life." This sense is the opposite of feeling like a passive spectator, of lacking direction.

Society conditions us to do and to have. It does not condition us to *be*. Yet our identity comes from our *be*ing. If we are identifying with what we do, and something prevents us from continuing to do it, then our identity is gone. If we have been identifying ourselves through what we have and we lose what we have, we lose our identity at the same time as we lose our possessions.

Identity is experienced from the inside out, not the outside in. The way that I am able to experience from the inside out is to experience as fact that I am *more than* everything I do, have, and experience. Reminding myself that I am *more than* each experience empowers me to make choices, expand my horizons, and move forward.

*But by the grace of God
I am what I am.
1 Corinthians 15:10*

Remember always that you have not
only the right to be an individual;
you have an obligation to be one.
You cannot make any useful contribu-
tion in life unless you do this.

Eleanor Roosevelt

Ask children who they are and they point to their bodies. It seems our bodies provide our first sense of identity. Some of us get stuck in that identity longer than others.

For more years than I care to admit my identity was my freckles and red hair. I thought that freckles and red hair were the worst things that could happen to anyone. No one told me I was cute, let alone pretty; I was always "Freckles" or "Carrottop." When I looked in the mirror, that was who I saw. No one told me I was more than my physical appearance, and I did not have enough sense to figure it out for myself.

A most gorgeous woman was in one of my classes. She had flawless skin and long, dark, thick lashes. Since I have invisible lashes and freckled skin, those are qualities I really admire. As I expressed my admiration to her one day, she said, "Yes, but look, I have this mole right here." My hunch is that every time she looks in a mirror she sees her mole, not her beauty.

After trying every freckle cream on the market, I still have my freckles. I also know now that I am a lot more than my freckles. When I thought of myself as my freckles and red hair, I was unhappy and unsuccessful. That identity robbed me. When I realized that I am more than my physical appearance or my physical being, I got my power back.

Yes, you have a physical state of being and appearance, *and* you are more than that physical state.

And let the beauty of the Lord
our God be upon us . . .
Psalms 90:17 (KJV)

I am the only person that fools me into believing I am less of a person than I am.

James Walt

For the first thirty years of my life I was unconscious, although I did not know it at the time. Looking back, I see it was as though I was in a deep sleep. As I began to awaken, I began to experience life.

Up until that time I had merely functioned. In fact I functioned rather adequately in some ways. As a housekeeper, for example, I knew the best brand of wax to buy and I had every towel folded perfectly in the closet. I functioned adequately as a seamstress, cook, and gardener. Those are predictable roles in which one can function fairly well while unconscious.

Functioning as a wife and mother (which were my principal roles) wasn't too predictable. All I could bring to these roles was my preconceived notion of what a good wife and mother was. (These preconceptions precluded my experiencing my roles in a meaningful way, since my ideas were rather narrow and didn't allow for much spontaneity.)

When I started to become conscious of being more than my roles and functions, I began to experience a new sense of self. I realized that I had existed before I was a wife and before I was a mother; therefore, those roles were not all I was. Being more than my roles enabled me to experience more freedom and creativity and to function more effectively in those roles.

My role of mothering is over and I still exist. I am glad that I knew that I was more than a mother before my boys left the nest so that my identity was not shaken once they were gone. I still play the role of wife and I love it. Experiencing that role as not who I am empowers me to bring more to my relationship with my husband.

Many people are drawn to my classes when their roles or functions change. They come in feeling lost. When they become conscious of being more than their roles and functions they get back their power to create a full life.

So God created man in his own image, in the image of God he created him; male and female he created them.
Genesis 1:27

23

What lies behind us and what
lies before us are small matters
compared to what lies within us.
Ralph Waldo Emerson

In class one night a woman announced that she was a "foodaholic."
I asked her if that was who she was, or if that was the way she
behaved. She looked puzzled and said, "Is there a difference?" She
hadn't separated who she was from what she was doing.

While conducting in-service workshops for schoolteachers, I ask
the teachers if they see their students as the students' behavior.
Usually about 75 percent of them say they do.

I explain that if a student is his behavior, then he has no power to
be different. For instance, I continue, we all have a need for
recognition. If a student does not receive recognition for positive
behavior, he may develop negative behavior to get the recognition.
Either way the behavior is learned and can be unlearned. "The
student, you, and I are all responsible for our behavior," I conclude,
"and since we existed before we behaved the way we do, that is not
who we are. Being more than our behavior, we can control it rather
than let it control us."

When I see myself or others as our behavior, I limit us all. When I
see us as being more than our behavior, I see the power to change
that behavior.

Yes, you are responsible for your behavior, *and* you are more than
your behavior.

. . . I will strengthen you, I
will help you.
Isaiah 41:13

24

A life spent in making mistakes
is not only more honorable but
more useful than a life spent
in doing nothing.
George Bernard Shaw

Show me a person who has failed at something and we will be looking at a person who has achieved something. Success and failure are as linked as roses and thorns. Failure demonstrates that an attempt has been made. People who are attempting things at least win admiration for their efforts.

Yet I encounter many people who are frozen with fear of failure. They have an unrealistic picture of themselves, of others, and of life itself. Remember, Thomas Edison and Babe Ruth failed more times than they succeeded, yet we honor them for their successes. Looking at successful men and women and seeing how many times they had to fail before they found success might help us transform our assessments of ourselves.

For the first thirty years of my life I played it safe, didn't fail at much, and didn't succeed at much. Since then I've become experimental and attempt a lot. I sometimes fail and I often succeed.

When I fail at something I acknowledge the failure and then tell myself I am more than the failure. It is awareness of being more than the failure that empowers me to keep on keeping on.

Ever feel like a failure? Remind yourself that while you are responsible for your failures, you are more than those failures.

> *. . . I will lead them in paths*
> *that they have not known . . .*
> *Isaiah 42:16 (KJV)*

We are dominated by everything with which our self becomes identified. We can dominate, direct, and utilize everything from which we disidentify ourselves.

Roberto Assagioli

While out of town on a speaking engagement I wrote several vignettes for this book. I had been home for two full days, and my husband had made no effort to read them. His reading them was important to me, and I felt deeply hurt by his apparent lack of interest. Knowing, intellectually, that I—and not Larry—had created the hurt, I began to look more closely at the situation.

During the two days I had been home, Larry could not have been a more loving and attentive husband. As a woman I could ask no more; as "my work" I felt rejected. I could hear my inner voice saying, "I am my work." Unconsciously I had been identifying with my work. If I was my work and Larry wasn't giving his attention to what I had achieved, that explained my pain. Yet Larry did not marry my work; he married *me*, the woman.

I reminded myself that I had existed and had married Larry before I chose to write about my work. I was *more than* my work. My work was important to me, *and* it wasn't who I was; it was one way I expressed myself.

After all this had become clear to me the hurt was gone. Have you found it as much of a challenge as I have to establish your identity from the inside out?

For what person knows a man's thoughts except the spirit of the man which is in him?
1 Corinthians 2:11

SELF–ESTEEM

As soon as you trust yourself, you will know how to live.
Goethe

If society were different, we might be
content just to do something well. But
no one is pleased to simply do what they
do. What's important for us is always
what doesn't exist.

Joseph Johns

Julie, from one of my teen classes, had not been doing very well in school. Her mother told me that she had discovered that her daughter was writing her papers and not turning them in. The girl's reason for not turning in her papers was that she had not finished them. Her mother added that her daughter was a perfectionist and that everything had to be just right or she wouldn't have any part of it.

"Suppose you came to my house and told me you were hungry and that your favorite sandwich was ham and cheese on rye," I said. "Then when I went to fix the sandwich I found I had only ham, cheese, and whole-wheat bread. Would you then refuse to eat?"

"No," she responded. But it was clear that that was exactly what she was doing in school.

One of the biggest surprises I ever had in conducting classes was working with a group of CETA participants. These were people who had not been able to get or hold jobs. I discovered that the majority of them were perfectionists who had let their perfectionism immobilize them. Like Julie, if they couldn't do well, they wouldn't do anything at all.

Some people use their perfectionism to drive themselves to the top, while others are paralyzed by it. In either case they are victims of low self-esteem. They are always focusing on what they don't do rather than on their accomplishments.

Before leaving class one evening a very successful woman related some of her shortcomings to me. Looking directly into her eyes I said, "You really aren't good enough for yourself, are you?" Her eyes welled up with tears and she murmured, "That's what I've been saying to myself, isn't it?"

Are you good enough for you?

If God is for us, who is against us?
Romans 8:31

Enlightenment is the absence of comparison.
> Paul Brenner, M.D.

Jean was a tall, willowy brunette with flawless skin. She sat before me looking miserable and told me that other women made her feel inferior.

"Jean, how do other women make you feel inferior?"

"Well, my chin recedes a bit, and my breasts are flat. My hair is too curly . . . " and she recited a long list of "flaws."

"Jean, do you always compare yourself to other women?"

"Yes, I do, and there is always someone prettier."

"When you find someone with features you would like to have, does that mean you are not OK as you are?"

"Of course."

Like Jean, many of us make ourselves feel inferior or inadequate by comparing ourselves to others. If we've been feeling pretty good about ourselves, this is a sure way to bring ourselves down. There will always be someone around more talented, more intelligent, better educated, better looking, wealthier, more successful than we are.

I explained to Jean that for a long time I, too, had made myself miserable by making comparisons. However, I'd decided I had suffered long enough. Now I look at people as flowers, each one unique. Roses can't be like buttercups, or daisies like thistles. Each has its own beauty and its own niche to fill. "The choice is yours," I said. "You can continue feeling inferior by comparing yourself to others, or you can accept and enjoy your own uniqueness. Just know that you are creating your own feelings either way."

Which feelings are you creating?

> *Having gifts that differ according*
> *to the grace given to us, let us*
> *use them.*
> *Romans 12:6*

*Wherever there is a human being
there is a chance for kindness.*

Seneca

Recently a letter was returned to me because of insufficient address. As I examined it, I realized that I had left a zero off the house number. A zero! The letter was returned for lack of a zero. I began to reflect upon the zero, and how frequently it is referred to as "nothing."

Yet the zero is really essential in life. Programmers would have to develop a whole new language for the computer if they lost the use of the zero. Adding machines and calculators are useless without zeros.

Occasionally I encounter people who think of themselves as zeros, who are convinced they have accomplished nothing in life. Perhaps this is because they have not recognized their own value and have remained unaware of how important they are to others. How important is a friendly smile when you feel all alone? Or a good home-cooked meal when you are hungry? A tender touch when you are sad? Or companionship when you are lonesome? Listening may not seem important; still, ask the person on the receiving end what it can mean.

Ever feel like a nothing, a zero? Remember: Zeros, too, are important. Enough zeros after a single dollar would make us all billionaires!

*And He said, "Truly I tell you, this
poor widow has put in more than all
of them . . . "
Luke 21:3*

30

*What makes men good is held by some
to be nature, by others habit or
training, by others instruction. As
for goodness that comes by nature,
this is plainly not within our control,
but is bestowed by some divine agency
on certain people who truly deserve to
be called fortunate.*

Aristotle

Occasionally I find a person who wants to participate in one of my classes and cannot do so for financial reasons. Sometimes I am willing to invest in people and encourage them to participate, with the agreement that they will pay when they can.

I made this offer to one woman who became far more successful in her business after participating in the classes and began to achieve recognition in her community.

This woman never paid me anything, and I suppose her guilt bothered her. Every time we met she said, "I feel so bad because I have not paid you anything." Over a two-year period this statement was repeated to me several times. Finally I inquired very softly, "Do you want to know why you feel bad?"

"Yes, why?" she responded.

I said to her, "You gave your word and you haven't kept it."

She is a mirror for me. Every time I give my word and don't keep it, I feel bad. This does not have to be over something major, like a financial obligation. It can be as simple as saying, "I'll drop you a line" and not doing it. When I become conscious that I've given my word and not kept it, I correct the situation as soon as possible. Then I can feel good about myself again.

How do you feel when you've given your word and not kept it?

*Whatever you have to say let your
"yes" be a plain "yes" and your
"no" be a plain "no."*
Matthew 5:37 (JBP)

*If you accept your own limitations
you go beyond them.*
Brendan Francis

As a human-growth educator, I sometimes feel that I am one of the most fortunate people in the world. My students teach me far more than I teach them because they share with me their thoughts, conflicts, and frustrations. And as they do, I often begin to see patterns emerging. A pattern that I see consistently is one where people focus on getting their needs met by others, rather than focusing on how they can meet their own needs.

As people confide in me what they want in relationships—whether it's acceptance, respect, love, or forgiveness—I usually find that these same people are unwilling to give to themselves what they are expecting from someone else.

I know that in my own personal life, when I quit rejecting some part of me and accept myself as I am at the moment, I am no longer overly concerned about whether someone else accepts me. When I am willing to love me and take care of myself, I no longer demand that someone else love me or take care of me. This does not mean that I don't want others to love me; it only means that I am not crushed when they don't.

Are you demanding that someone give you what you are unwilling to give yourself? Try giving to yourself what you really want or need. See if it is still so important that you receive it from someone else.

*For I, the Lord your God, hold your
right hand; it is I who say to you,
"Fear not, I will help you."
Isaiah 41:13*

LIVING IN THE NOW

Men spend their lives in anticipation, in determining to be vastly happy at some period or other, when they have time. But the present time has one advantage over all other; it is our own.

Charles Caleb Cotton

I have known a great many
troubles but most of them
never happened.
                    Mark Twain

During a telephone conversation my seventy-year-old mother said, "I just dread getting old more and more every day."

"Mom," I replied, "you are living getting old twice. Once when you get there, and once now."

Thoughtfully she said, "I guess you are right."

I suggested that once was enough, that she could deal with being old when it happened.

When my boys were younger we frequently got into discussions about what they were going to do when they were in high school. Some of their ideas made me panic, and I tended to start my standard lecture. I finally realized I was crossing bridges before I came to them. Once I came to that realization I responded to their "When I'm in the tenth grade . . . " with, "If you still want to do that when you get to the tenth grade, we'll talk about it then." It was amazing how that reduced my anxiety and eliminated a lot of unnecessary discussion.

I've learned that I create my own anxieties by trying to live my future now. I do that by playing "What if": What if we have a war? What if we have a depression? What if there's a hurricane? What if I lose this contract?

When I give up this game and live today today, peace and tranquillity return. I still have my long-range goals and plans for my future. I simply do today's work toward their achievement.

Are you playing the "What if" game and trying to live your future today?

Don't worry at all about tomorrow.
Tomorrow can worry about itself!
One day's trouble is enough for
one day.
Matthew 6:34 (JBP)

*We cannot know our future, but
we can surely destroy our
present by dwelling on our
past.*
> Author unknown

A common game we can play to spoil our here and now is the game called "If only."

Linda was in a deep state of depression. She sat in my office playing this game: If only she had been a better mother her children would have turned out better. . . . If only she had been a better wife she would not have lost her husband to another woman. . . . Her list went on and on. She was immobilized by her guilt and self-hate.

During our conversation she mentioned her religious faith several times. I asked her if her faith did not teach that she was forgiven for her mistakes. "Oh yes," she replied. "The Lord has forgiven me, but I haven't forgiven myself."

Very gently I took her by the hand and said, "When Linda is too good to forgive Linda, it really doesn't help to have a forgiving God." She stared at me in disbelief. "Linda," I continued, "you've been acting more righteous than God. He has forgiven you for being human and you haven't forgiven yourself. Did you know how to be a better wife and mother at the time?" She shook her head no. "Then of what are you guilty?"

Linda began to see that she had created her own hell. Before she left my office she went through the process of forgiving herself.

Is there anything for which you need to forgive yourself?

> *Where God grants remission of
> sin there can be no question
> of making further atonement.*
> *Hebrews 10:18*

When it is time to die, let
us not discover that we have
never lived.
Henry David Thoreau

Have you ever been driving and discovered that you have passed through some little town and not noticed it? That's what I call being unconscious. A lot of us go through the trip of life that way. We don't notice the little towns, we don't have any trouble along the road, and we don't experience the pleasure of the moment.

Years ago I saw a cartoon showing a grave marker with these words inscribed: "Here lies the body of John Doe, who died at the age of 39 and was buried at the age of 72." That cartoon spoke to me. Being unconscious is like walking around dead.

I am amazed at how many things I can perform unconsciously. Some things I even do fairly well. There is not really anything *wrong* with this kind of unconsciousness; we just miss a lot of experiences. For instance, have you ever eaten a meal and left the table feeling unsatisfied? You probably weren't present when you ate. Being conscious means being present in the moment. That is how we experience our experiences.

Experiment with your next meal. First really look at it. Experience your food with your eyes. Then smell it. What does it smell like? Now taste it. Chew each bite several times and notice how the flavor increases with each chew. Savor it. Enjoy it. Notice the pleasure you derive from food. See if you need as much food as usual to feel satisfied. Did eating consciously make a difference?

I still act unconscious a lot. When I notice I'm doing it, I remind myself to come back to the moment. As you focus your consciousness on the here and now, notice how rapidly you expand your awareness. Pay attention to the difference in the quality of your experiences.

Awake, O Sleeper . . . and Christ
shall give you light.
Ephesians 5:14

The danger of the past was
that men became slaves. The
danger of the future is that
men become robots.
Erich Fromm

Awareness is a key to growth and power. To raise my awareness I created an imaginary observatory in my head. I started observing both my inner and outer worlds, even started using the word *observe* in conversation so that my mind would keep hearing the directive. Concentrating on being aware made me ask myself, "What am I aware *of*?" That question turned on the equipment in my observatory.

Traveling to a nearby city to conduct a workshop, I observed men in the field harvesting maize. I became aware of the thought, "I know all about maize." The observer in me said, "What do you know?"

Startled and stammering, I replied, "Daddy raised maize when I was a little girl. The men itched a lot during harvest. We fed it to the chickens." That was all I knew. A few minutes before my thought had been, "I know all about maize." My familiarity with maize had made me think I knew all about it. Laughing, I began to wonder in how many other aspects of my life I thought I knew all about something simply because I was familiar with it. Learning more about maize did not change my life; seeing the difference between familiarity and knowing did.

Do you want to raise your awareness? Create an imaginary observatory and imagine yourself as the observer.

But blessed are your eyes,
for they see, and your ears,
for they hear.
Matthew 13:16

*Nothing is there to come, and
nothing past, but an eternal
now does always last.*
Davideis

Ten-year-old Heather, with her freckles and big, brown eyes, sat across from me looking somewhat nervous. She was there because she was not doing well in school, although tests had shown that she was very bright. We talked for awhile about her school work and I told Heather I had a hunch about why she wasn't doing well. After a brief silence she asked what my hunch was. I said, "My hunch is that your body goes to school every day and your mind goes someplace else."

She lit up like a light bulb and said, "I think you are right."

"Heather," I asked, "where does your mind go?" She rolled her eyes around and said she didn't know. I said, "Heather, if you don't know, who does?"

She rolled her eyes again, thought a minute, and said, "It goes home."

I then asked her to close her eyes and imagine her body sitting in a classroom without a mind. A minute later she opened her eyes and said, "That's awful."

Again I asked her to close her eyes, and this time to imagine her mind at home without a body. Her eyes popped wide open and she exclaimed, "I've been splitting myself up!"

I directed her to close her eyes again and this time to imagine going after her mind and bringing it back to where her body was. "That feels so much better," she said.

I told her that her mind would probably continue to run off and that every time it did she was to go get it and bring it back to where her body was. I wanted her to experiment with that for a week and to call and let me know if it made a difference. One week later I received her call. Enthusiastically she told me, "Boy, does my mind run off a lot! I had to go get it all week. It really made a difference—I made 95s, 98s, and a 100."

Thank you, Heather, for reminding me to keep my mind where my body is.

*This is the day which the Lord has
made; let us rejoice and be glad in it.*
Psalms 118:24

MIND AND ATTITUDES

The greatest revolution of our generation is the discovery that human beings, by changing the inner attitudes of their minds, can change the outer aspect of their lives.

William James

As the plant springs from, and
could not be without, the seed,
so every act of a man springs from
the hidden seeds of thought and
could not have appeared without
them.

James Allen

One of the things I learned growing up on a farm is that you can't plant corn and get okra. When you want corn you plant corn; when you want okra you plant okra. That is how seeds and soil work.

I am convinced that is also how thoughts, images, and minds work. Thoughts and images work like seeds and the mind works like soil. Thoughts and images held in focus begin to germinate, take root, and grow into reality.

Years ago I had a secretary who was on a weight-loss diet. Frequently I would hear her say, "I'm just a little fatty."

After three weeks of the diet she complained to me one day that she had lost very little weight. I asked her if she really wanted to lose weight.

Shocked, she blurted out, "Of course I do! Why do you think I'm on this diet?"

"Kathy, I hear you say to yourself several times a day, 'I'm just a little fatty.' You are giving your subconscious mind two instructions. One to lose weight, one to stay fat. In addition to your diet, you might want to start planting thoughts of slimness."

She agreed to experiment with thinking slim and imagining herself weighing her ideal weight. The following week she reported losing four pounds.

My mind is a marvelous enabler when I'm clear and plant the ideas and images that I want it to produce.

What kind of thoughts and images are you planting in your mind?

As he thinketh in his
heart so is he.
Proverbs 23:7 (KJV)

The mind is its own place,
and in itself can make a
heaven of hell, a hell of
heaven.
John Milton

One night I turned the TV to a late-night talk show and there, being interviewed, was the renowned family therapist Virginia Satir. She made the statement that one of the attributes of the mind is that it cannot stand not knowing. So when it doesn't know something, it makes things up.

I was fascinated by this idea and began to check my thoughts. It didn't take me long to observe the truth of her remarks.

One of my treasured relationships had been somewhat strained for some time. I sent my friend a note inviting her to lunch. Two weeks went by with no acknowledgment. I kept wanting to make things up about why I had not heard from her. What I seemed to make up was not complimentary to me or to her. When I noticed that I was doing this, I announced to myself that I was making up reasons and that the truth was that I did not know why I had not heard from her.

Finally I received a note from my friend. She was in another state, dealing with a serious illness in her family. Nothing I had wanted to make up was even close to the truth. That was a valuable lesson.

Some of the things I made up as a child, when I didn't have all the available facts, were still running my life. For example, I had decided that my value and worth as a person depended upon other people's opinions of me. One of my biggest challenges is to uncover all that I've made up and not make up anything new. When I become aware that I am making something up, I say to myself, "Bobbi, you just don't know, so don't make anything up; wait and get the facts."

Are you aware when you are making things up?

The Lord will perfect that
which concerneth me.
Psalms 138:8 (KJV)

Compared to what we ought to be,
we are only half awake. We are
making use of only a small part
of our physical and mental
resources.

William James

When I started out in the motivational business in 1964, most authorities agreed that we used between 10 and 15 percent of our potential. More recently Dr. Jean Houston of the Mind Research Center in New York has stated that the average person uses no more than 10 percent of his or her physical potential and 5 percent of his or her mental potential. That's not very much considering that we have 90 to 95 percent sitting there unused. I began to ask myself, "If that is the case, why is it so?" I came up with several possible reasons.

Some of us don't want to be different. I remember when I was in the eighth grade I liked English grammar. Attending a country school where speaking correct English was definitely not the "in" thing to do, I learned to butcher the language as well as everyone else. Our need for acceptance and approval is one reason we don't explore our possibilities.

Another reason we don't use our potential could be that we don't know that it exists. Until Roger Bannister ran a four-minute mile, that feat was thought to be impossible. Since Bannister broke the four-minute barrier, many other athletes have done the same.

Also, we don't really need to use more of our potential to survive. Most of us are "getting along" just fine the way we are.

Psychologist Fritz Perls thought that the main reason we don't use our potential is that we get stuck in our old habits of thinking and reacting. I suspect that is indeed the principal reason.

Every expert agrees that we all have much more potential than we are utilizing. What is keeping you from using yours?

As each of us has received a gift,
employ it . . .
1 Peter 4:10

I've known countless people who
were reservoirs of learning
yet never had a thought.
        Wilson Mizner

An idea that has disturbed me for some time now is that people are taught *what* to think, yet most of us are not taught *how* to think.

My parents loved me very much and really wanted the best for me, so they taught me what I was to think and believe—and that I was not to question. Also, as far as I can remember, my teachers were the same way: "This is the way it is, so don't question." The other major influence in my early life was my religious affiliation, and at church too I was told exactly what to think. As a result of all this, I accepted as fact that I was not to think or question, and I was a nonthinker for more years than I care to admit.

As I began to mature emotionally I began to give myself permission to think. Believing there is a spirit within us with clear perception, I began to question: Is there another way to look at this? In what other ways can this be so? How else can this be viewed? I imagined the situation or point in question in the center of a large room, with me walking in a full circle around it, seeing it from a series of different perspectives. As a result life has really become far more interesting and exciting.

Are you accepting other people's thoughts as yours, or are you thinking for yourself?

> *But the counselor, the Holy*
> *Spirit, whom the Father will*
> *send in my name, he will teach*
> *you all things . . .*
> *John 14:26*

*Speak the affirmative, emphasize
your choice by utter ignoring of
all that you reject.*
　　Ralph Waldo Emerson

The man's voice on the cassette tape was giving instructions on how to develop both sides of the brain. With my eyes closed I was focusing on following his directions. At one point he directed the listener to focus on the right side of the brain and not to think about the left side. Until he instructed me not to think about the left half of my brain, I was not even conscious of having one. Once he had told me not to think about it, the left side dominated my consciousness.

This reminded me of all the times I had said to myself, "I am not going to do that again"—really determined not to repeat an act—and then had gone back and done it again. Sometimes I've instructed my mind not to think certain thoughts any more. That never works. The first thing I know I'm thinking exactly the way I do not want to think.

We don't erase old thought patterns except by replacing them with new, more desirable patterns. When our mind does not know what we do want, it doesn't know what to do.

Changing behavior and attitudes is the same way. When our attention is focused on negative behaviors or attitudes, that is what we experience. When we really shift our attention from the undesirable to the desirable behavior we can start experiencing the new, more effective behavior or attitude.

Do you want to change an old behavior or attitude? Decide on a new one. Imagine yourself achieving the desired results, and then watch them come into being.

*Take the offensive—overpower
evil with good!*
Romans 12:21 (JBP)

Success doesn't come to you.
You go to it. You don't buy
it with Green Stamps. There
is no paycheck until the work
is done.
                    Marva Collins

In my classes I ask the question, "How many of you have been told that all you have to do is believe?" The majority of the hands go up. The next question is, "Has it worked?" And the answer is no. When we think that all we have to do is believe, we "fold up our wings" and wait for something to happen.

Many experts believe in and teach the value of good nutrition. After some study of the subject, I believe good nutrition is essential to good health. Believing in good nutrition while eating junk foods does not make my body healthy.

Other experts preach the value of exercise. After listening to these authorities and looking at their evidence, I, too, believe in the value of exercise. However, believing in exercise has not helped the shape of my body, my energy level, or my cardiovascular system. Until I "get off it" and get my body moving, the belief will not benefit me.

We have many beliefs about ourselves, life, other people, and God. Some of these beliefs are valid, some are not. Belief is essential in a lot of things. Alone it is not enough. Action is also necessary.

Belief opens the door to possibility. Action takes us through the door.

So faith by itself, if it has
no works, is dead.
                    James 2:17

Liberty of thought is the
life of the soul.
                    Voltaire

When I was going through one of the more difficult times in my life, I was employed by a business college. One morning my employer said to me, "Bobbi, I don't know how you maintain such a good attitude under your present circumstances."

"It's simple," I said. "Every morning when I get up I say to myself, 'You have a choice. You can let this get you down, or you can rise above it.'"

"When you put it that way," he said, "you don't have much of a choice."

"When I put it that way, it is easy to choose."

Man's Search for Meaning by Viktor E. Frankl taught me about choices. From him I learned that my right to choose is the only thing in life that cannot be taken from me.

I did not always know about choices; I consider Frankl's lesson one of the most valuable I have ever learned. Giving myself choices, even in insignificant matters, makes a difference. For instance, one inner dialogue I have goes like this: "You can enjoy the pleasure of this pie for ten minutes and then feel lazy and fat, or you can do something else pleasurable to keep your mind off the pie and keep you feeling good." Decisions become easier when the choices are clear.

When Al enrolled in my class he had been miserably unhappy for a number of years. After a discussion in class about choices Al came back the following week as excited as a small boy on Christmas morning. He eagerly reported how learning about choices had turned his life around—how by giving himself a conscious choice in every situation he had turned his work environment into a happy, productive place for both himself and his employees. He said, "It's amazing how something so simple is so powerful!"

Do you look for your choices in your life?

He shall eat curds and honey when
he knows how to refuse the evil
and choose the good.
Isaiah 7:15

46

Experience is not what happens
to a man. It is what a man
does with what happens to him.
Aldous Huxley

At a small dinner party one night the conversation turned toward fasting. Three people at the table practiced fasting on a fairly regular basis, and they were all expounding on what they perceived as its benefits. After this discussion had gone on for awhile one of the men said, "I went nine days without any food while I was in Korea, and I certainly don't ever want to do that again."

I thought about that statement for quite some time. I remembered the times I had to miss a meal for some reason or another and how I had reacted. I usually felt very deprived, physically weak, and really hungry by the time of the next meal. Then I thought about the times I *chose* to skip a meal—or meals—when on a fast, and how differently I felt, both mentally and physically.

Having to go without food and *choosing* to go without food are entirely different experiences. I've thought about this often since and observed how true it is in all facets of our lives. I've been making an effort to change my "I have to" to "I choose to," and I've found that I have a lot more energy as a result.

How about you? Do you have any "I have to" that you can change into an "I choose to"? I bet you'll be surprised at the resulting difference in your energy level.

Each one must do as he has made
up his mind, not reluctantly or
under compulsion . . .
2 Corinthians 9:7

47

*Judgments are our personal ego
reactions to the sights, sounds,
feelings and thoughts within our
experiences.*

W. Timothy Gallwey

A number of years ago I read a book listing words that were judgmental. I was surprised at how many judgments I was making without realizing it. The discovery really motivated me to think about the effects of making judgments. While progress has been slow, I've at least learned to recognize when I'm being judgmental, and the consequences. Judgments block learning from—and acceptance of—what exists and create emotional reactions that have consequences in themselves: guilt, defensiveness, immobility.

To become nonjudgmental, as I've come to understand it, is to see clearly and add nothing to the facts. It does not mean ignoring flaws, errors, and mistakes; it simply means not adding anything to them.

I have been using the game of pool to observe my judgmental attitude. I make a shot, the ball goes where I want it, and I judge it to be a good shot. In the excitement of a "good" shot, I don't observe what I did so that I can repeat it. I make another shot, it misses the goal entirely, and I judge it to be a "bad" shot. Because of the judgment I don't observe what I did so as not to repeat it. A pool shot just *is.* The ball goes where I would like it to or it doesn't, and if I am busy judging the action I'm not likely to find pleasure in the game or to learn anything from it. This has been an enlightening experience and a pleasant way to work at being nonjudgmental (with the fringe benefit that my pool game is improving). I am working to take this experience and apply it to myself, my job, and my relationships.

How do judgments affect you?

Judge not that you be not judged.
Matthew 7:1

*A man who reforms himself has
contributed his full share towards
the reformation of his neighbor.*
                    Norman Douglas

One of the best investments I ever made was attending a work-shop with Dr. Dee Mundschenk. I came away from that workshop with one idea, an idea that gave me back my personal power.

There were thirty-six people in our group, each one a mirror for me. Every time one person complained about what someone else was doing or not doing, Dr. Mundschenk responded with, "What they are doing is not the issue. The issue is, how are you letting their behavior affect you?"

After hearing this said in a number of different ways throughout the day, I finally got it. I finally saw my reflection clearly. I had been using my power to try to get other people straightened out. Since that didn't work, I was left feeling frustrated and powerless.

I finally realized on a deep level of consciousness that I had no real power to straighten out others. The only real power I have is over *me*. When I began to spend my energy straightening *myself* out, my feelings of helplessness were transformed into feelings of personal power.

How are you using your power?

> *. . . first take the log out of your
> own eye, and then you will see
> clearly to take the speck out of
> your brother's eye.*
> Matthew 7:5

Perspective . . . use it or
lose it.
Richard Bach

As an observer of human behavior, I find it interesting to see the different ways people react to the happenings in their lives. For example, I know two college students who both failed the same course. One student and her family reacted to this failure as though it were a catastrophe. Much of their mental and emotional energy was spent dwelling on how bad this was and how adversely it could affect her future. The other student regretted that he had not taken the course as seriously as he might have, and that as a result he was going to have to go to school during the summer to make it up.

One viewed the situation as catastrophic, the other as a passing inconvenience. As I reflect on things that have happened to me in the past, I realize I viewed many as catastrophes at the time that, in retrospect, were merely passing inconveniences.

Now when I start getting uptight about things not happening the way I want them to, I'm learning to ask myself, "Will this be a catastrophe, or is it a passing inconvenience?" The tension subsides as I realize it is just an inconvenience.

How are you seeing the unwanted situations in your life—as catastrophes or passing inconveniences?

> *. . . let not your hearts be troubled,*
> *neither let them be afraid.*
> *John 14:27*

The ways in which a man accepts
his fate and all the suffering it
entails . . . gives him ample opportunity—
even under the most difficult circumstances—
to add deeper meaning to his life.

Viktor E. Frankl

While visiting a home for drug abusers, I met a young man named Adam. "Adam," I said, "I really like your name."

He replied with a chip on his shoulder, "I don't know why, it just means dirt."

"Isn't that great!" I responded.

"You're kidding. What's good about dirt? Because of dirt I have to take baths and wash my hair and my clothes."

Remembering when I had first seen him, I said, "Adam, awhile ago I saw you walking around barefooted on the good green grass. I love to do that, too. We can do that because of dirt. Also, Adam, because of dirt we have all the beauty of nature, all the food we eat, and planet Earth on which to live." Adam looked at me, shocked: he had never thought about the good in dirt, and my hunch is he had not thought about the good in Adam, either.

Granted, when dirt is in the wrong place it can cause problems. However, the good it brings into our lives far outweighs the hassle. Which do you emphasize, the good or the trouble? They are both there. I have been taught—and I believe—that whatever we emphasize we multiply. I am not suggesting that you overlook the hassles in life. I *am* suggesting that you deal with them and emphasize the good.

What have you been emphasizing?

. . . whatever is true, whatever
is honorable, whatever is just,
whatever is pure, whatever is
lovely, whatever is gracious, if
there is any excellence, if there
is anything worthy of praise, think
on these things.
Philippians 4:8

Everybody wants to understand painting.
Why is there no attempt to under-
stand the song of birds? Why does
one love a night, a flower, everything
that surrounds a man, without trying to
understand it all?

Pablo Picasso

Ruth was really stuck. The course was nearly over and there was no evidence that she was making any progress. My plan was for her to come in to see me privately.

In telling her story she kept repeating over and over again that she did not understand why she wasn't getting ahead at work and why she was so very unhappy. She accompanied her drama with a sigh and shrug of the shoulders, as though she had given up.

"Ruth," I inquired, "do you think you have to *understand* what's happening to you before you can do anything about it?"

She repeated defensively, "I just don't understand how I've gotten myself into this mess."

My somewhat impatient reply was, "Ruth, do you have electricity in your house?" She nodded yes.

"Do you understand how electricity works?" She shook her head no.

"So you don't have to understand electricity to benefit from it. Ruth, insisting on understanding is a cop-out. I sense you are unwilling to *do* anything to make your life work."

I knew what Ruth was doing. When I did not want to experience life the way it was, I thought it to death trying to understand it. I shared this insight with Ruth. By the time she left she had decided on a plan of action.

Yes, I still like to understand *and* understanding doesn't change the facts or circumstances. Are you too stuck in the need to understand something to *do* something about it?

Trust in the Lord with all thine
heart; and lean not unto thine own
understanding.
Proverbs 3:5 (KJV)

52

If there was nothing wrong in the
world there wouldn't be anything
for us to do.
George Bernard Shaw

A young girl whose father had recently died was sharing with me some of her anger about this loss. She ended by saying, "It just isn't fair." I agreed with her that she had gotten a rotten deal. I could see how hard it would be to lose a father at an age when you really need him. The girl kept repeating, "It's just not fair." I asked her if she thought life was supposed to be fair, and she replied, "Yes, of course it is."

I hesitated, then explained that I had lived for quite some time, and found that life was not always fair. For instance, was it fair for one person to be born with great mental ability so that learning came easily, while another person really had to work at it? We discussed this and other "injustices" that she had not thought about. She acknowledged that she could see it wasn't fair that in some ways she had so much and some of the kids in school had so little. I said, "Yes, and as you accept the fact that life isn't fair you can recover from your loss."

Sometimes life deals us a rather difficult hand—a hand that truly seems unfair. When this happens, it is up to us to decide how we are going to react and how we will play out the hand. We can walk around shaking our head and saying, "It's just not fair," or we can take the hand we've got, get on with the process of living, and perhaps pick up some wild cards along the way.

How are you playing the hand life has dealt you?

For he makes his sun rise upon evil
men as well as good, and he sends his
rain upon honest and dishonest men
alike.
Matthew 5:45 (JBP)

God grant me the serenity to accept
the things I cannot change, courage
to change the things I can, and
wisdom to know the difference.
Serenity Prayer

Why. It's a small three-letter word, and when it's used in the scientific and business world it can lead to the investigation of reasons or causes and promote discovery and creativity.

On the other hand, "why" as a constant approach to life can become immobilizing. Why me? Why did it happen? Why did they do that? These kinds of questions reflect an attitude that keeps a person caught inside a problem.

I am chagrined to admit how much of a "why" person I was until a friend got my attention by telling me that asking why all the time was a big cop-out. Stunned into silence, I did a lot of thinking about "why." Soon I realized that when I did not want to face reality and deal with my life, I asked why things were that way. Suddenly I could see that asking why was usually a way to avoid what *is*.

Soon I learned to face facts by asking "*How* can I deal with this? *What* can I do about it? *Where* can I find the solution? *When* am I going to do something about it?"

Why keeps me bound up in a problem or a situation. How, what, where, or when lead me toward a solution.

Ask, and it will be given you;
seek, and you will find; knock,
and it will be opened to you.
Matthew 7:7

SELF-UNDERSTANDING

The only conquests which are permanent and leave no regrets are our conquests over ourselves.

Napoleon Bonaparte

There is properly no history;
only biography.
    Ralph Waldo Emerson

History became interesting to me when I began to study the human nature behind events. Since human nature doesn't seem to be changing very much, history keeps repeating itself. And until we start to learn from history, I suspect it will continue to repeat itself just as we, as people, continue to repeat our life patterns.

A young mother I know kept herself upset. Much to her embarrassment, she cried when crying wasn't appropriate and experienced a lot of anxiety. I suggested that she keep a journal for a week and record all the events in her life and the feelings that accompanied them.

Together we went over her journal and discovered that she was never present in a single situation. When something was happening she had mentally already gone on to the next event. She came to realize that the attitude underlying this behavior was her sense that she had to hurry up or she would not get through with her daily work. As we studied her history, she realized that she had felt hurried ever since she was a child. This awareness helped her concentrate on staying in the here and now, and she began to change the course of her life.

Another student of mine had recently gone through a divorce. Her most frequent complaint against her former husband was his self-pity. I watched her interest develop in another man; he got her attention by getting her sympathy. It is common for a person to marry someone with qualities similar to those of his or her former spouse. Until we study our lives and look at our own part in shaping them we will probably continue to repeat the same scenes with new characters.

By studying my own history, I have freed myself to change my life patterns. Are you studying your own personal history?

And be renewed in the spirit of
your minds.
Ephesians 4:23

I will not be concerned at other
men's not knowing me; I will be
concerned at my own want of ability.
Confucius

Pat, a sixteen-year-old girl who had run away from home a week earlier, was seeking a way to return home—*and* save face.

She sat before me pouring out all her reasons for leaving home. Then she concluded, "They just don't understand me."

"Pat," I responded, "it sounds to me as if you don't understand *yourself*. Do you?"

"No, I don't," she replied.

Gently I asked, "Pat, if you don't understand yourself, how can you expect your parents to understand you?"

She thought about that for awhile.

"Pat, I've discovered that occasionally other people know me even better than I know myself. There are parts of me that only I can know; there are parts of me that others can see that I don't recognize; and there is a part of me that is simply unknown.

"It sounds to me like you want self-understanding. That takes time and effort. A good way to start is to listen to your own thoughts and observe your own behavior. Listen to your parents and others to see if they can mirror for you a part of yourself that you have not recognized. Consider their opinion carefully and try to notice if there is any truth in it. This can get you started on knowing and understanding yourself. As you come to understand yourself, it won't be so important what your parents do."

She smiled and asked to use the phone to call her parents to come for her.

Have you been seeking understanding from the wrong source?

There is a spirit in man; and
the inspiration of the Almighty
giveth them understanding.
Job 32:8 (KJV)

58

Our opinion of people depends less
upon what we see in them than
upon what they make us
see in ourselves.
                          Sara Grand

In psychiatry, projection is the unconscious act of ascribing to others our own ideas or impulses. We tend to assign to others both our negative and positive characteristics.

A young college student told me how the guys she met were always letting her down. I asked how they were doing that. As she talked we discovered that she formed a romantic, idealistic picture of each guy. After some time, when she discovered he didn't conform to the image she had constructed, she blamed him rather than looking at how she had set him—and herself—up.

My husband and I had been married a short time when I asked him if he felt unable to express his anger at someone he loved. He said he did not feel that way at all. I felt sure that he did and would not admit it. Three months later I finally admitted to myself that *I* was the one who felt that way, not he.

When we have traits that don't fit our concepts of ourselves we sometimes deny them in ourselves and assign them to others. When Wanda was in her graduate counseling program, she got very angry and impatient working with clients who had addictions to alcohol and drugs. Her supervisor asked her what *her* addiction was. With indignation she replied, "I don't have any."

Later Wanda was able to recognize that her anger and impatience were rooted in her addiction to food. She had put on forty pounds since her husband's death. When she admitted her addiction, she found that she could work with her clients more easily.

Without exception every trait that has ever bothered me about someone else, I possess. It usually takes me awhile to admit it. Once I do, and I start to clean up my act, the other person doesn't bother me anymore.

Do you want self-understanding? Allow others to be your mirror.

> *. . . I shall understand fully even as I have*
> *been fully understood.*
> *1 Corinthians 13:12*

59

Sickness is a kind of warfare
within the body; health the
result of peace within our
beings.
            Dr. David Seabury

After scheduling time off from work and reserving a place to write, I was very disappointed to awaken ill during my first night at my retreat. My entire upper respiratory system was affected.

For two days I merely existed. Truly believing that every illness contains a message and that sickness can be a result of internal war, I began looking for conflicts. It didn't take me long to find them. The previous week had been an unusually hectic one. Knowing I was to be in town only one week, I had been torn much of the time between what I could get done and what there was to do.

I had also been torn between staying with my writing style or changing to one offered by a professional critic. I decided to follow my gut feeling. Still, that caused stress for several days.

The major conflict occurred Sunday when I was really torn between staying home with my husband and meeting some of his needs and my plan to get away and finish the book. I suspect if I had recognized the seriousness of this conflict and discussed it with Larry I could have released the stress and avoided the illness.

I eventually resolve my conflicts, although sometimes they have to create enough stress to produce illness before I even know I have them. Are you feeling torn by conflicting desires? Pay attention to them before "dis-ease" sets in.

> *... Let everyone be fully*
> *convinced in his own mind.*
> *Romans 14:5*

We are handicapped by what
we think we can't do.
                    Mark Twain

Our feelings of inferiority and inadequacy started with the S.O.B.s
that we grew up with: the shoulds, oughts, and buts.

When we were little people, our parents and the others who
loved us wanted what was "best for us," so they told us we *should*
do this and we *ought* to do that; we *shouldn't* do this and we *ought
not* to do that. Naturally we believed them. After awhile the shoulds
and oughts became "the truth," and we too began to *should* on
ourselves and others. These shoulds and oughts formed the ideal
pictures of how we should be. When we did not fit our parents'
ideal pictures, we sometimes received these messages: "I love you,
but"; "That is really good, but"; "You are a neat person, but . . . "
We began to develop the idea of conditional love and acceptance,
and we began to feel inadequate and inferior.

As adults we still find that others have ideal pictures of us. We
can react by getting angry because they *shoulded* on us, or we can
be even more irrational and feel inadequate or inferior because we
don't fit their ideal pictures. Another option we have is to recognize
that other people are imposing their pictures on us. We can let it be
OK that they have a picture of us—and that we don't fit their
picture.

Feeling inadequate or inferior is a signal reminding us that we
still have an ideal picture in our head that we are not achieving.
Recognizing that we also impose these S.O.B.s on others and being
aware that they are counterproductive burdens, we could decide to
give them up.

Are you willing to give up your ideal pictures? We really can
accomplish as much and do just as well without them—and so can
our children and spouses.

Do not be conformed to this world
but be transformed by the renewal
of your mind . . .
Romans 12:2

Every man has a rainy corner in his life from which bad weather besets him.

Jean Paul Richter

One of the young men in a training seminar I was conducting for a large company came into class early. He began to tell me that both his parents were alcoholics. I suggested he stay after class that evening so that we could have a "pity party," just he and I. I asked him if he had ever been to a pity party.

Blushing a bit he said, "*Yes, but* I had not recognized it before."

Another man in the class, the company comptroller, told me about his early background. His parents were extremely poor and he had not learned any of the social niceties or had the cultural advantages that his position demanded. He told me that he could handle the job itself well; it was the social expectations that were immobilizing him. I invited him to join our pity party.

Both men stayed after class. I explained that to have a successful "pity party" all we had to do was really talk about how bad our lives were. None of us would give any advice or suggestions for making life any better; we would only offer pity.

While both men had legitimate reasons for self-pity, it only took about forty-five minutes for them to recognize how useless that self-pity was. Both left the "party" with some ideas on how to get on with their lives.

Do you have reason for self-pity? Give yourself a good pity party, then get on with your life.

. . . in all these things we are more than conquerors through him who loved us.
Romans 8:37

FEELINGS

The door to the human heart can be opened only from the inside.

Author Unknown

Emotions are always the result
of a given perception and
interpretation.

John Powell

During my childhood and youth the role models in my life were busy surviving a depression and then war. In that environment emotions seemed like weaknesses. I frequently heard such remarks as, "You've got your feelings on your sleeve," "Feelings are a weakness," "Be big," "Be strong," and "You shouldn't feel that way." My interpretation of these messages was, "Maybe I shouldn't feel what I feel, and if I do I must never let my feelings show." Changing that conclusion and learning to value and experience my feeling nature has required much work and rethinking on my part.

Now I've come to think of our feelings as our sixth sense. We experience our outer world through our five senses, and our inner world of thought through our feelings. For example, imagine you are awakened in the middle of the night by a very loud noise. Your first conscious reaction is fear. However, preceding the fear comes the unconscious thought, "What is it?" When you determine the source of the noise and discover that it is not a threat, your fear dissipates. The fear is a direct sensory response to the thought, "What is it?"

Once I understood that feelings are a sensory response to thinking and once that concept penetrated my unconscious mind, I finally began to experience my feelings. What was surprising was the new surge of energy and freedom I felt.

Feelings add extra dimension and richness to life. Are you allowing yourself to experience that richness?

> *... a time to weep, a time to*
> *laugh; a time to mourn, and*
> *a time to dance ...*
> *Ecclesiastes 3:4*

*Although the world is very full
of suffering it is also full of
overcoming it.*
                    Helen Keller

Many men and women who participate in my classes have ca-
reers and are active in their communities in meaningful and rewarding
ways. They are willing to take a lot of chances, and as a result they
experience a lot of success. Ironically, these same people are sometimes emotional cowards, afraid to become involved because they
think they will be hurt. When we experience this fear we are
expressing an unconscious belief that in getting hurt we will be
permanently harmed. As a result we are not really participating in
intimate relationships; although we have surface relationships, we
are afraid to get really close to others for fear we will be hurt. Those
closest to us might die or leave us, for example.

I've had my share of deep hurts. At the time they felt as though
they would last forever. I remember how losing someone important
to me left me feeling empty inside. Though I wouldn't have believed
it at the time, the hurt was not permanent—nor was I harmed by it.
It showed me everything was working right in my system.

Some hurts I have experienced for an unreasonable length of
time because I kept rubbing salt into the wounds by reliving the
experience over and over again in my mind, and by insisting that it
never should have happened. With no salt in the wound and a little
time, hurts heal without any permanent damage.

Once I realized that I did not need to experience harm just
because I hurt, I opened myself up to genuine intimacy. As the
thorn goes with the rose, hurt often goes with love.

Are you willing to hurt? If you're not, you will hurt permanently
from loneliness; if you are, you are free to experience love and joy.
Remember: You can experience hurt without being harmed.

*Blessed are you that weep now,
for you shall laugh.
Luke 6:21*

*I have always felt sorry for people
afraid of feeling, of sentimentality,
who are unable to weep with their
whole heart. Because those who do
not know how to weep do not know how
to laugh either.*

Golda Meir

A young woman with whom I was working was describing some events in her life and some of her deepest feelings. As she related these experiences, I was moved to tears. This was a total shock to her. As I began to question her shock, she said to me, "You are strong and you have it together; you are not supposed to feel." Now it was my turn to be shocked. I acknowledged to her that I, too, considered myself a strong person and thought I "had it together" to some degree. I didn't see how that had anything to do with my ability to feel.

Since then a number of people have verbalized their belief that strong, successful people do not experience feelings like hurt and sadness. They think such feelings indicate weakness. Actually people who "have it together" have the same capacity to feel pain, sadness, or hurt as those who don't. In fact, one must have the capacity to experience pain in order to have the capacity to experience joy. What we feel is never a weakness; what we *do* about what we feel can be a sign of a weakness. The person who "has it together" may have the same feelings as the person who doesn't; he just handles his feelings differently. One handles them in a positive, constructive way, the other in a self-destructive way.

How are you handling your feelings?

*And when he drew near and saw
the city he wept over it.*
Luke 19:41

Anger ventilated often hurries
towards forgiveness; anger concealed
often hardens into revenge.
Edward G. Buliver-Lytton

Gloria had gone through a divorce about two years before enrolling in one of my classes. She was still stuck in her anger and had not been able to put her life back together.

During her private time with me she said that she would like to tell her former husband the way she really felt.

"Sounds like you have not done that," I commented. I asked if she was ready to do it right then and there.

She hesitated, squirmed a bit, then said, "It wouldn't do any good."

"*Yes*, you are right, it will not change the facts, *and* it will do you some good to get it out of your system. This is a safe environment here and we are going to place this chair in front of you so you can imagine your former husband sitting there. You can tell him everything you have ever wanted to say. Call him anything you want."

With some prompting she began to verbalize all the hurt and anguish she had been experiencing. Between her sobs her voice rose to a high pitch of emotion. She vented her blame and self-pity. She called him a few choice names. When there was nothing left to say she looked at me with her eyes wide open and exclaimed, "I can't believe how good I feel!" Placing her hand over her chest she continued, "I have had a physical pain right here for months; I haven't been able to release it. Now it's gone. I don't understand how this has worked."

"You don't have to understand it, because you have just experienced it. Just enjoy your freedom."

I don't really understand the magic that comes from expressing our pent-up negative emotions, although I have personally experienced it and I have observed many others go through transformations with this technique. If you have been holding in feelings, experiment with this method, and experience the release.

Let all bitterness and wrath and
anger and clamor and slander be
put away from you, with all malice.
Ephesians 4:31

It is better by noble boldness to run the risk of being subject to half of the evils we anticipate than to remain in cowardly listlessness for fear of what may happen.

Herodotus

A salesman I knew had an important client to call on, yet he kept putting off making the appointment. He told me that he had to develop better work habits. My hunch was that the problem wasn't poor work habits; rather, it was fear of rejection by the important client that caused him to delay the call.

I asked him if he was afraid his client would say no. His response was, "I guess I am. I'm afraid he won't buy."

My next question was, "If he doesn't buy, will you feel rejected?"

"Yes," he responded, "I always feel rejected when people tell me no."

I then asked him, "Are they rejecting *you* or are they rejecting your service? There is a difference, you know." He looked surprised that there was a difference. He had been taking the rejection of his services as a personal rejection.

As I reflected on the incident later, I thought about all the things that never get said or done because of people's fear of rejection. When we realize that someone can say *no* to our requests, suggestions, or ideas and still say *yes* to us as people, maybe we will be willing to risk more. Will you?

And which of you by being anxious can add one cubit to his span of life?
Matthew 6:27

How much more grievous are the consequences of anger than the causes of it.

Marcus Aurelius

A man named Joe was among my acquaintances. Joe was a man I really disliked; he was a very vindictive person who said things like, "I know that God says vengeance is His, but he needs me to help Him out." I shuddered when I heard that pronouncement and all his other declarations about how he was going to get even with various people. I really could not imagine myself as a vindictive person.

I thought my reaction to Joe was based on my strong belief about vindictiveness being a destructive way to deal with anger. Can you imagine my shock when I became aware that I was withholding love from a person because I felt he had caused me pain? My vindictiveness was so secretive that even I had not recognized it! Once I did, I decided to express my anger in an open and direct way that would allow our relationship to continue. When we don't have permission in our own heads to express anger directly, it takes other forms. Vindictiveness is one such form.

The healthiest thing we can do with our anger is to express it directly in a nonthreatening way, not accusing or blaming the other person involved. It's *our* anger. We created it, so we need to express it, without blame.

Angry with my husband, I said, "Larry, I love you, and right now I am feeling really angry with you." He looked at me, smiled, and said, "And it's OK, isn't it? It's OK to be angry with me as long as you love me." Expressed, the anger was gone, and only love remained.

It really is safe to express your anger, if you express it without attack or blame. People usually know we are angry anyway. Expressing it clears the air.

Be angry but do not sin; do not let the sun go down on your anger.
Ephesians 4:26

70

*A splendid freedom awaits us when we
realize that we need not feel like moral
lepers or emotional pariahs because we
have some aggressive, hostile thoughts
and feelings toward ourselves and others.
When we acknowledge these feelings we no
longer have to pretend to be that which
we are not.*

Joshua Loth Liebman

Up until his dad's death the year before Mike had been a model
student and had had good relationships both at home and at school.
Since his father's death he had been in constant trouble. I had a
hunch he was displacing his anger, so I "went fishing."

"Mike, if I were thirteen and my dad died when I needed him
most, I would be mad."

"I am," he said, dropping his eyes and head, "but God took him."

"If God took my dad when I really needed him, I would be mad
at God."

Barely whispering, "I am."

"Have you told God that you are mad at Him?"

"No, He would strike me dead."

"Mike, God knows you are angry with Him and He understands.
You just need to talk with Him about your anger so that you can get
over it."

Like so many of us, Mike did not feel safe about being angry with
God, so he displaced his anger. He considered it safe to act out his
anger at school, where he didn't have as much to lose.

To everyone's relief, Mike was able to face and resolve his anger.
His mother reported that he was soon his old self again.

Probably all of us know someone who is pleasant, kind, and
considerate until he gets behind the wheel of an automobile. Then
a personality change occurs; our mild-mannered friend curses out
half the drivers on the road in language that is completely out of
character.

Like Mike, this person doesn't think it is safe to be angry with
whoever is the real target. So he directs his anger toward someone
in whom he has no emotional stake.

71

Are you dealing with your anger directly, or are you displacing it?

> *... he was hungry. And seeing a fig tree in leaf, he went to see if he could find anything on it. When he came to it, he found nothing but leaves, for it was not the season for figs. And he said to it, "May no one ever eat fruit from you again."*
> Mark 11:12–14

Hearing is one of the body's five
senses. But listening is an art.
                    Frank Tyger

While lunching with a friend one day I was conveying to her a
very strong feeling about something that was going on in my life.
She gazed into space and said, "I wonder what that is all about." I
felt depersonalized, as if I were a problem in a textbook. The other
feeling I had been discussing became secondary, because at that
moment I felt fury. I was glad that our lunch was almost over.

Determined to figure out why I felt such rage, I looked back at
the history of our friendship. She had been a very supportive friend
in many ways. She was someone I really cared about. As I began to
study the relationship, I remembered the other times I had been
just as furious with her. Each time it had happened when I was
sharing my feelings. Her pattern was always to diagnose or analyze
my feelings rather than to acknowledge them.

Could this lack of acknowledgment, I wondered, be the reason so
many people don't share their feelings?

Aha! That was it. I did not want a diagnosis or analysis. I only
wanted to *share* the feelings. Seeing my friend as a mirror, I
promised myself that day that I would acknowledge people's feelings before I offered them anything else. I had experienced how
important it was to be acknowledged and what it felt like when I
wasn't.

On another occasion I was feeling down over a situation and
related this feeling to a different friend. His response was, "That's
kind of hard to take, isn't it?" All he did was acknowledge my
feeling—and I felt release, and affirmation as a person.

Are you analyzing or acknowledging other people's feelings?

> *Let thy ear be attentive and*
> *thy eyes open.*
> *Nehemiah 1:6*

RELATIONSHIPS

The meeting of two personalities is like the contact of two chemical substances: if there is any reaction, both are transformed.

Carl Jung

Examine the contents, not the bottle.

The Talmud

Among those attending a weekend workshop I conducted for secondary educators were a priest and a nun, both dressed as laymen, with nothing to set them apart physically from the group. I soon observed that some students in the group set them apart anyway.

On Friday I had spent quite a bit of time talking with the priest. He asked me if I had any trouble seeing him as a person. I smiled, because I understood his question, and said, "No, I'm aware of you as a human being. Having chosen to be a priest does not exclude you from the things that other people feel and experience." He told me how difficult it was for people to relate to him as a person; most related to him only in his role as a priest.

On Saturday I asked the sister if she had the same problem in her relationships with people. Pointing to a young man in the group, she said, "Oh yes. In fact, he can't stand my being here without my habit. He has expectations of what I'm supposed to do and say and how people should respond to me, and he becomes terribly upset when it doesn't work that way." She went on to say that wasn't unusual, and that it definitely was a problem.

Since then I've been reflecting on how we often put a person in a role and how we have certain expectations we associate with that role. Then we become upset or disappointed when he or she doesn't live up to the role and fulfill those expectations. I see this most frequently in husband-and-wife roles, although it's really universal. How are you seeing and responding to others? In the role you have created for them, or as people?

There is neither Jew nor Greek,
there is neither slave nor free,
there is neither male nor female,
for you are all one in Christ
Jesus.
Galatians 3:28

Maturing is the process by which
the individual becomes conscious
of the equal importance of each
of his fellow men.
                    Alvin Gaeser

At a party one night a woman came up to me and said she had been reading my newspaper column. Then she remarked, "You sure have a lot of interesting friends." Because of the way she said it, I wasn't sure if she believed they really existed. She was a somewhat older woman, and surprised me with her aliveness, vitality, and youthful enthusiasm. Before the evening was over, she became one of the interesting people I know.

Remembering this later and feeling very fortunate about my friends, I commented to my husband on how lucky I was to have so many interesting people in my life; I just knew I was the luckiest person around. His response surprised me. He said, "Bobbi, the people you meet are the same people everyone else meets; people are interesting to you because you are interested in them."

This reminded me of the story about a man arriving in a new town who asked a local resident what kind of town it was. The wise resident replied by asking the newcomer how it was where he came from. The newcomer explained that he had found the people cold and unfriendly. The resident replied, "You'll find them the same way here." The resident knew that the man's attitudes would determine the way he saw others.

How are you experiencing the people who come into your life?

So let us concentrate on the
things which make for harmony,
and on the growth of one another's
character.
Romans 14:19 (JBP)

77

The deepest craving that we have
is the craving to be appreciated.
William James

An attractive, well-groomed woman in her mid-forties sat in tears as she poured out her story. Her marriage was breaking up. It was obvious that she was in pain and that she did not want that to happen. She began to tell me what a terrific fellow her husband was. She recited a long list of his virtues and told me how much she admired and respected him. I could not see what had gone wrong, so I asked her.

She really broke down then and said, "All I've ever done is complain and find fault with him."

I asked her if she had ever told him that he was a terrific fellow.

"No," she replied, "I was afraid it would go to his head and he would leave me. If he knew how great he was, he sure wouldn't want me."

I sat for a moment stunned by her reasoning—or perhaps by the lack of it. Then I became preoccupied for a moment, wondering how many people withhold genuine praise or appreciation for fear that it will "go to the other person's head" and result in their being rejected.

Returning to the situation at hand I noted that the woman's fault finding and criticism had obviously not worked. Since at this point she had nothing to lose, I suggested that she might want to go home and tell this "terrific fellow" the truth, exactly what he really did mean to her. She did, and they eventually worked out their problems.

Do you ever withhold praise or appreciation? We all need that acknowledgment, and we seek out people who will fill that need.

Enter his gates with thanksgiving,
and his courts with praise!
Give thanks to him, bless his name!
Psalms 100:4

Love consists in this, that
two solitudes protect and
touch and greet each other.
 Rainer Maria Rilke

While visiting another city, I met a woman who from all appearances had everything going for her. She was attractive and talented, with a charming home and what seemed to be a stable family life. She was also extremely depressed and unhappy in her marriage. She told me how she and her husband had met, how they had cared for each other, and how they used to be able to talk for hours. As she described the way they were when they had met eight years before, they both sounded like really exciting, vibrant, fun-to-be-with people. As she described her husband now, he didn't sound very interesting, and certainly not exciting. And as I listened to her complain, it was obvious that she, likewise, wasn't either.

I offered a suggestion as to what she might do to revitalize the relationship. Her response was, "I have my pride."

Driving back to Corpus Christi I was reflecting upon this comment when I realized that it's generally not the "other woman" or the "other man" that is a threat to a marriage; it's boredom, and apathy. I asked myself, "If I were my mate, would I want to come home to me? Would I find me interesting, exciting, or even pleasant to live with?" These questions jolted me into seeing my responsibility to my relationship with my husband. I hope they are enlightening to you as well.

. . . comfort one another . . .
1 Thessalonians 4:18

Unless you give up your resentment
to your parents you remain as a
child.

Fritz Perls

A woman was leaving class one night when she turned at the door and said, "I am forty-eight years old and I recognized for the first time tonight that I am still trying to get my mother's approval."

During another discussion a young woman described how much her mother's expectations had influenced her feelings of low self-esteem. Everything her mother had said might have been proclaimed by God himself.

In his book *The Language of Feelings*, Dr. David Viscott states that "Parents are simply people who happen to have children." I have thought about that statement a lot, and I shared it with the young woman. I asked what her attitude would be if she looked at her mother as an *equal*, a person just like herself, rather than as her mother. She thought about that very carefully and replied, "Really very different. As a person, I could see her with understanding and acceptance." I suggested that she might want to experiment with seeing her mother as an equal for awhile and see if their relationship changed.

As children we see our parents as omnipotent, all-knowing and all-wise. If they fail us, we think they have done it deliberately. We don't see their humanness, the limits of their wisdom, their insecurities, or their pain. Often we carry this attitude into our adult lives. Becoming conscious of the humanness of my parents has caused me to view them as people who have had their own experiences to deal with: pain, failures, and triumphs. This realization has allowed my expectations of them to fall away, along with the expectations I held for myself as a parent.

How about you? How are you seeing your parents, and how is that view affecting your life?

. . . all of you are children of
the most High.
Psalms 82:6 (KJV)

We are all so much together, but
we are dying of loneliness.
Albert Schweitzer

Have you ever been together with someone and yet not really been *together*? I'm sure we've all had that experience on occasion. The sad thing is that for some people this experience is a way of life. They share the same space, eat at the same table, and never tune in to each other emotionally.

Carolyn was suffering from emotional malnutrition. Her husband was a highly successful corporate executive who worked ten hours a day. When he came home he would eat, discuss business, and then go to his room to read so that he could keep current on business and world affairs. His withdrawal caused Carolyn to withdraw also. As I gathered information about their backgrounds it became clear to me that as children neither of them had adult models who knew how to be attuned to them. Not surprisingly they hadn't learned how to tune in to others.

Togetherness is not achieved through quantity of time. It's achieved through quality of time. We have to change our self-concern to concern for another, at least long enough to put ourselves in the other's place and give some evidence that we understand what he or she is experiencing. That's togetherness.

When I have experienced togetherness the result has been a strong feeling of well-being. When someone has been very attuned to me and let me know it, that creates music for my soul. When I feel as if I've been so attuned to someone else that I've been inside that person, I feel warmth and closeness. It takes a lot of work, and it's worth every bit of the effort.

Are you being together with someone without really being *together*?

For this reason a man shall
leave his father and mother
and be joined to his wife,
and the two shall become one
flesh.
Matthew 19:5

*You give but little when you
give of your possessions. It
is when you give of yourself
that you truly give.*
              Kahlil Gibran

A frequent complaint I hear is that someone meets a lot of people, but that when he encounters these people again they don't remember him. Some people have enrolled in my classes specifically because they want to be remembered by others. I generally find that they themselves are very difficult to get to know. They want to be remembered, yet they haven't recognized that they must give of themselves in order to *be* remembered.

Several years ago my husband and I spent a weekend at a small resort with four couples we did not know. Through some close sharing we got to know each other well. One man began to relate some very personal conflicts with which he was struggling. As he told of his inner struggle, our whole group felt warm and supportive. This sharing opened the door for the rest of us to reveal something of ourselves.

When Sunday evening came, none of us wanted to break the closeness and go our separate ways. Reflecting on the weekend I marvel at how close we all felt, simply because we were willing to share of ourselves and our inner worlds. It is not likely that we will ever forget one another.

The people I do forget are the people I never really get to know. Do you want to be close, to be remembered? Try revealing a part of yourself.

*The point is this: He who sows
sparingly will also reap sparingly,
and he who sows bountifully will
also reap bountifully.*
              2 Corinthians 9:6

I have never met an aggressive person who wasn't a fearful person.

John Bradshaw

Have you ever known someone you began to feel a little close to, then had that person jab you with one of his thorns? That generally ends the closeness.

When I take the jabs personally, as though what was done was done specifically for the purpose of hurting me, I spend a great deal of time picking out the thorns. My first inclination has been to avoid the presence of a thorny person. Now I'm learning to look beyond the thorns. It appears to me that the person who jabs the most is the person who is most afraid of genuine closeness; his jabs are nothing more than a method of self-protection. When I can see the person protecting himself I don't take the jabs personally.

A woman related to me how much of a failure she was as a wife. Her husband was unhappy with her most of the time. I inquired how her husband got along with the rest of his family and in his business. It became obvious that she wasn't the only one getting jabbed by his thorns.

"Do you feel personally responsible for your husband's unhappiness?"

"Yes, how else can I take it? He says that it is my fault."

"Didn't you say your husband wasn't speaking to several members of his family?" She nodded. "You also said he had trouble keeping good employees because of the way he treated them." Again she nodded in agreement.

"It appears to me that your husband is unhappy in most of his relationships. If that is so, I don't think you have to take his unhappiness personally."

People do what people do because that's what people do. Sometimes we are there while they do it. Most of the time their behavior is the same whether we are there or not.

... having compassion one of another ...
1 Peter 3:8 (KJV)

The only thing we have to fear is
fear itself.
Franklin Delano Roosevelt

Along with all the pleasures that come from living in the beautiful "Sparkling City by the Sea" comes the threat of hurricanes. During one such threat, while the storm's exact destination was still unknown, I found it interesting to study human behavior under stress. I observed panic, fear, and conflict. Some people said they felt guilty for praying that the hurricane would go somewhere else. I also observed a growing communal closeness, supportiveness, helpfulness, and caring.

I myself felt calm in this time of possible threat, primarily because it was the first time I had ever charted the path of a hurricane on a weather map and listened to the official weather bulletins. Rumors of all sorts could be heard just about every place I went. Every time I heard a rumor like "It's coming here," I would go back and look at my map to see the direction the storm was actually traveling. I soon knew that it was not in fact moving in our direction.

As I reflected on what various people had told me the storm was going to do, I concluded that people often hear what they fear. As I thought about this I realized that it is often true in personal relationships, too. People sometimes hear rejection from someone because they fear rejection. Some hear criticism when criticism isn't intended, because they fear criticism and can't deal with it.

What do you fear? Is there a real basis for it? How often do you actually experience what you fear? Could you have interpreted events to coincide with what you feared or expected? Consider that you could be hearing what you fear rather than what was meant.

For I, the Lord your God, hold
your right hand; it is I who
say to you, "Fear not, I will
help you."
Isaiah 41:13

COMMUNICATION

The only gift is a portion of thyself.
Ralph Waldo Emerson

I know you believe you understand
what you think I said but I am not
sure you realize what you heard is
not what I meant.
            Author Unknown

In a workshop for communicators conducted by John Grinder and Judith Delozier I learned that their theory was, "There are no mistakes in communications, only outcomes." That was a rather profound statement and I've thought a great deal about it since.

One evening I was with a small group of women discussing some of the things that were said to us when we were little and how we let them affect us. I remembered that when I was in the sixth grade my cousin was a substitute teacher for my class. I felt anxious to be good and wanted to impress her. However, when it was my time to read aloud, I read very poorly. When class was over she came up to me and said, "Bobbi, you really can't read very well, can you?"

In my mind the "voice of authority" had spoken; what she had said was fact. The outcome of that communication was that I became a nonreader. I read only what I had to until I was thirty years old. This was about the time I began reexamining and discarding some old programming. I discovered that I liked to read and since have become an avid reader.

Looking at the outcomes of some communications I've received motivates me to be more careful about the communications I send. I have observed that every one of my communications certainly does have an outcome. Sometimes it is close to what I have intended and sometimes it isn't. When it isn't, my challenge is to find ways to communicate again and get the outcome I intended. What kind of outcomes are you getting?

> *Be not rash with your mouth,*
> *nor let your heart be hasty . . .*
> *Ecclesiastes 5:2*

But, if I tell you who I am,
you may not like who I am,
and that's all that I have.
John Powell

Grace is a gorgeous, talented, and successful young woman, prominent both socially and professionally. She had just fallen head over heels in love with her idea of Mr. Perfect.

She came to see me because she was scaring herself into believing she was going to lose him. I asked her on what she was basing her fear.

She said, "I've told him the truth about me. I don't wear my sophisticated and successful mask around him. I've told him what I really like and dislike, and even my self-doubts and insecurities."

"Grace, that is beautiful."

Tearfully she said, "*Yes, but* suppose that's not what he wants. What if he wants someone who is really sophisticated and self-assured?"

"Grace, if you wore your mask and played a part, and he fell in love with the mask and part, would you ever feel totally loved?"

"Not really," she sobbed.

My evaluation: "You have taken a chance. If he loves the you that is, then you will truly feel loved. Are you willing to settle for less?"

Hesitantly she said, "I guess not, but it would sure hurt to lose him."

"Yes," I said, "and it would hurt more having him love what you are not."

Have you ever scared yourself by revealing the truth about yourself? Have you taken the risk and found it worth it?

Therefore confess your sins to one
another, and pray for one another,
that you might be healed.
James 5:16

88

The prickly thorn often bears
soft roses.

Ovid

Nina was in one of the first classes I taught. At first I experienced her as a cynical, aggressive, aloof person. As I got to know her I recognized that her behavior was a facade that covered up a very caring and vulnerable core. We became friends, and that friendship has grown and deepened over the years. Even though we are separated by distance now, we still arrange to have time together once or twice a year. She has made a great contribution to my life and is one of the people who inspired me to write this book.

The last time she was visiting me we were reminiscing about the beginning of our friendship. "Nina," I said, "it took me awhile to see through you. You really are a pussycat, a very warm and loving person."

She smiled a pleased smile and said, "I guess that is one reason we are such good friends. You can see through me."

After she had gone home I remembered her last comment and wondered how many of us present ourselves to others as though we were an open book that says, "Here I am, read me!"—all the while knowing that the pages of our book are blurred. Our fantasy must be that other people can somehow read our minds.

Like Nina, we could have a long wait for understanding—until we are willing to reveal what we want other people to know.

A gentle tongue is a tree
of life . . .
Proverbs 15:4

89

There are two things to aim at in life;
first, to get what you want; and, after
that, to enjoy it. Only the wisest of
mankind achieve the second.
　　　　　　Logan Pearsall Smith

A big gray cat named Stray sleeps by the door to the cottage where I am staying to write this book. Every time I go in or out the door Stray asks me to stroke her. I usually slip my shoe off and stroke her several times with my foot. She is fun to watch because she lets me know just what she likes and turns in every direction so that she gets stroked all over. She is usually very content after a little stroking and I don't hear any more out of her until I go out the door again.

One day, eager to get down to the river, I ignored Stray as I passed her. She wasn't about to put up with that and was loud and persistent in her meowing. I came back, took my shoe off, and gave her some good strokes with my foot.

Stray gets attention from me because she asks for it. Being aware of what I was doing and why, I remembered one of my students who told me recently that she wasn't getting her needs met by her husband. I inquired if she had discussed her needs with him; she dropped her eyes and said, "It doesn't mean anything when you have to ask for it."

Watching Stray purr during the stroking she had insisted on helped me know beyond the shadow of a doubt that there was no truth in the woman's statement. Stray had kept after me until she got what she wanted and was enjoying every minute of it.

Are you willing to take a chance and ask for what you want and what you need? Honest, it feels the same.

> *Ask and it will be given you;*
> *seek, and you will find; knock*
> *and it will be opened to you.*
> *For everyone who asks receives ...*
> *Matthew 7:7–8*

RESPONSIBILITY

Enter upon your inheritance, accept your responsibilities.
Sir Winston Churchill

Man is condemned to be free;
because once thrown into the world
he is responsible for everything
he does.

Jean-Paul Sartre

Many years ago I participated in a growth group. Each week we received evaluation slips letting us know the areas in which we could benefit by making some changes in our attitudes and behaviors. When we received the slips evaluating responsibility, mine, along with the majority of the group, revealed that we had "average" attitudes toward responsibility.

I was indignant. I paid my bills on time; I voted; I was prepared and showed up on time to conduct my classes. It took me a long time to realize there is a lot more to responsibility than those things, however important they are.

Being responsible, as I am coming to experience responsibility, is accepting as a fact that I am creating the experiences of my life. *What is* is. *What is* is neutral. You and I get to create our experiences from *what is*. That's good news, you see, because accepting that we are the creators of our own experience gives us the power to choose *how* we want to create our experience. Since I realized I was creating my world with a lot of pain and misery, I decided to re-create it in a more desirable state. I still mess things up sometimes. The difference is now I know that I do it. Accepting my responsibility gives me power; otherwise, I am the powerless victim of circumstance.

One area in my life where I was avoiding responsibility was the paper work it took to keep my office running efficiently. I avoided this responsibility for a long time by judging it unimportant. People were what was important. People are very important, and so is the running of my office. When I avoided the responsibility of my paper work I felt frustrated and irritated. As I scheduled time for the paper work I created an experience of tranquillity and satisfaction.

Are you happy with the life you are creating? If not, you can re-create it.

I can do all things in Him
who strengthens me.
Philippians 4:13

Liberty trains for liberty.
Responsibility is the first
step in responsibility.
William Edward Burghardt Du Bois

Josephine sat in my class, her enthusiasm filling the room. She exclaimed with gusto, "I have a switch that only has two speeds, on and off."

I responded with, "You know you did not come here with that switch. You created it. If it is not serving you well, you might want to re-create it as a variable-speed switch."

Lighting up, she said, "I never thought of that before. I can see my new switch now. It is just like the dimmer switch on my light fixture. I can go at any speed I want."

In that same class Jane remarked that she was a born worrier. I found it very funny to try to imagine a "worry baby," and I quipped, "Since most babies are born either boys or girls, I'll bet you sure attracted a lot of attention." She did not see it as humorous at all and went on to defend her contention that she was helpless to do anything about her worrying.

Both Josephine and Jane had expressed an attitude that is very common—the belief that the traits and characteristics people possess have been bestowed upon them by fate. Some people, like Josephine, don't *know* that they are responsible for creating their approach to life. Others, like Jane, don't *want* to be responsible.

Believing our experiences are ruled by fate puts us in a position of helplessness. Accepting responsibility for our lives gives us power.

Therefore lift your drooping
hands and strengthen your weak
knees, and make straight paths
for your feet . . .
Hebrews 12:12–13

*Most folks are about as happy
as they make up their minds to
be.*

Abraham Lincoln

All too often I hear the expression, "I'll be happy when . . . "

One young woman said to me, "I'll be happy when I get married." I asked her if she was happy now, and she replied, "No, but I will be when I have a husband." I expressed my conviction that if she wasn't happy as a person, a husband certainly couldn't make her happy. Besides, what a burden being responsible for her happiness would be for him! A husband could add to her happiness or he could detract from it to some degree, but he could not make her what she wasn't.

I shared with her that I, too, had nurtured the fantasy that I would be happy when all was right in my world and when I had the right person to share my life. Having lived many years without that happening, I finally realized that my problem was that I had not wanted to be responsible for my own happiness. I thought happiness depended upon external conditions and was therefore looking for another person to create my happiness.

Since external conditions weren't perfect for too long, and since no one showed up to make me happy, I finally made a decision that I would be happy and that I would be willing to be responsible for myself. Immediately my life was transformed. I allowed others to *add* to my happiness and not to be responsible for it. I even allowed some people to detract from my happiness, though not for very long.

The hardest decision is to be happy in spite of our world not being the way we want it.

What does your happiness depend upon?

> *But now I am coming to thee;
> and these things I speak in
> the world, that they may have
> my joy fulfilled in themselves.*
> *John 17:13*

94

EVERYDAY LIVING

The greatest, the most important of the arts is living.
Aldous Huxley

*If he is indeed wise he does not
bid you to enter the house of his
wisdom, but rather leads you to the
threshold of your own mind.*

Kahlil Gibran

I remember a teacher who had a very positive influence in my life. Her "thing" was Chinese proverbs. Each day she had a new proverb on the board, and quite often we discussed the great truth it revealed.

My favorite—and the one I remember best—is this: "Give a man a fish and he eats today. Teach a man to fish, and he eats forever." As an educator I make an effort to keep this thought uppermost in my mind. If I give all the answers, supply all the needs, I'm keeping the student dependent upon me. I really have faith that all people have within themselves everything they need to make their lives work. Conveying that faith and not giving a person the solutions to specific problems empowers the individual to find his own solution.

I had been talking with Sandra about her problem for about forty minutes. She kept asking, "What should I do?" Not having been successful in getting her to come up with her own solution, I suggested we switch roles. I would be the client. I would present my problem to her, and she could tell me how to handle it. In this role reversal she had an immediate solution. Her idea sounded like good advice to me, and I suggested that she take it. She left and we both felt good.

Many parents talk to me about their children. They say, "I've given them everything. I just don't understand why they won't do anything." Or "I've seen that they have everything they need. I just don't understand why they aren't motivated." Each time I hear these remarks I think, "Yes, you've given them fish, but have you taught them how to catch any?"

Are you giving away fish, or are you teaching people how to catch their own?

*And when he had ceased speaking,
he said to Simon, "Put out into
the deep and let down your nets
for a catch."*

Luke 5:4

Every problem contains a gift.
Richard Bach

When I ask John, a friend of mine, how things are going in his life and he replies, "I've had quite a few learning experiences lately," I know he is dealing with some problems. I enjoy this friend because of the way he handles his problems. His philosophy is, "There are no problems, only learning opportunities." John has motivated me to take this positive approach to my own problems.

When I say "problem" my body feels weary and my mind is focused on the negative. When I say "learning opportunities" my body feels excited and ready to go, and my mind is open and receptive. The results are very different. Looking back at my life my greatest growth has come about because of problems; each problem really did contain a learning opportunity.

Reflecting upon the value of problems, I remembered the naturalist who one day was watching a butterfly emerge from its cocoon. After watching the butterfly struggle for some time he decided to help it. He took out his knife and slit the cocoon enough for the butterfly to free itself. It fluttered around for a little while, then dropped to the ground, dead. You see, it is its struggle to gain freedom from the cocoon that helps the butterfly develop the strength necessary for flying.

Problems provide us with an opportunity to discover dormant talents and abilities of which we may be unaware. They contribute to our overall growth. How are you letting problems affect your life?

We know that in everything
God works for good . . .
Romans 8:28

Time cools, time clarifies:
no mood can be maintained
quite unaltered through the
course of hours.
 Thomas Mann

Have you ever been so happy and on such a natural high that you felt as though you could not contain yourself, or wondered how anyone could feel so good? It's a fantastic state to be in. When I am in this state I tell myself to enjoy it while it lasts, because it will not be permanent.

Life has pretty well demonstrated to me that nothing is permanent, that no state of being lasts forever. If I want to continue to be happy I will have to work at it. This continuous state of change also helps me to be aware of the fact that painful feelings are not permanent either. I can remember a time in my life when I hurt all the way to the core of my being and felt as though I had no life left in me. At the time I couldn't imagine that feeling changing. However, it did. It was not permanent either.

Are you suffering distressful emotions of any kind? Acknowledge the feelings. Allow yourself to really experience them, and at the same time remember that they are not permanent feelings. Are you experiencing happiness, joy, excitement? Allow yourself to really enjoy the experience and know that it, too, will not be permanent.

Rejoice in your hope, be patient
in tribulation, be constant in
prayer.
Romans 12:12

*For everything you have missed, you
have gained something else: and for
everything you gain, you lose something.*
Ralph Waldo Emerson

A friend once shared this philosophy with me: "You have to give up something in order to get something else." I had not heard that idea before. I thought about it for a few minutes and then dismissed it from my mind.

Later, as I was reaching for a second helping of ice-cream pie, her idea popped back into my mind. I realized how true her statement was in this instance; I had to give up that second helping of pie in order to maintain the weight I wanted. Then I began to reflect on other situations when we have to give up something in order to get something else. I could think of many instances when this idea applied to material things—like giving up the comfort of an old pair of shoes to have a more stylish pair, or trading in the old car we are still fond of to get a new model.

Though it was easy to see how the concept was applicable to the physical world, I began to wonder whether it also applied to emotional experiences. I thought about an acquaintance who had lost the love of her life. She was still holding on to that past experience. Until she could let it go, give it up, she would not be ready for a new love. We have to give up our resentments and hostilities to have peace and tranquillity. We give up despair to have hope, neutrality to have love, doubt to have faith, and on and on. What do you want in your life? What are you willing to give up in order to get it?

*And no one puts new wine into old
wineskins; if he does, the new
wine will burst the skins and it
will be spilled, and the skins will
be destroyed.*
Luke 5:37

God did not play dice with
the universe.
Albert Einstein

Not long after they reduced the speed limit from seventy miles per hour to fifty-five, I got two speeding tickets. I did not approve of the new law and just kept driving my own way. I knew I couldn't afford to get any more tickets or I would be in trouble with the insurance company, and maybe even endanger my driver's license. So every time I got in the car after that I said a little prayer and asked God to protect me. It wasn't two weeks before I got another speeding ticket. Sitting there stunned after the policeman drove off, I asked, "What happened, God? I have been asking not to get another ticket." The still, small voice within me answered, "If you don't want a ticket, don't speed."

So simple! I began to laugh at myself and my foolishness, and then started looking to see if I was breaking other laws in my life.

As I began to think about what laws are for, I first thought of the laws of the universe: the law of physics that states that energy cannot be created or destroyed; the law of gravity; the law of cause and effect. These are laws that govern the working of the natural world.

Then I began to wonder if life too didn't have laws that make it work. I thought of the Ten Commandments, and how they are referred to as the law. Certainly when we obey them our relationships run more smoothly. I suspect there are many kinds of laws, and that the purpose of all of them is to make things work. Our challenge is to look for the laws of life, and to live in harmony with them.

The law says, "Thou shalt love
the Lord thy God with all thy
heart, and with all thy soul
and with all thy strength and
with all thy mind—and thy
neighbor as thyself."
Luke 10:27 (JBP)

Affirmation of life is the spiritual act
by which man ceases to live unreflectively
and begins to devote himself to his life
with reverence in order to raise it to its
true value. To affirm life is to deepen, to
make inward, and to exalt the will to live.
Albert Schweitzer

Joy is one of the most alive people I know. Her eyes dance and she moves with enthusiasm. Occasionally she says, "Hooray for death!" I found her vivaciousness and that phrase incompatible. Each time I heard her say "Hooray for death!" I felt puzzled; every time I heard the phrase I attempted to see what truth lay behind it. I could understand "Hooray for the afterlife," though I didn't feel too eager to rush the experience.

One day the fog began to lift from my mind and I could finally see how death gives purpose to life. (If you don't believe that, imagine hearing that you only have six months to live.) Finally I could understand Joy's intense aliveness.

The concept of death makes us fully aware of life and of our strong desire to live. Thinking about my own death helped me to clarify my values. All too often I was making time for tasks more important than making time for relationships, doing more important than being. I was believing in spirituality rather than making time for spirituality.

When a situation arose that I felt irritated about, I would ask myself, "When my life is over, is this going to matter?" If the answer was no, then I could let it go. If it was yes, then I would put my energy into a solution. When there was more to do than I could get done, I would say to myself, "When my life is over and done, will this make a difference?" No. Hooray for death!

Frankly, I am amazed at how well I have survived without some things I once thought necessary, even without love from a person I had desperately wanted to have love me. Hooray for life!

. . . I came that you might have life,
and have it abundantly.
John 10:10

*Although the day is coming to an
end I feel that I have conquered.
I look for strength for tomorrow
so that I may start again.*
                    Michael P. Fenlon

A client was conferring with me about an employee who was behind in her work. My client, frustrated, said, "I've relieved her of phone duties, made sure she had no interruptions, and hired extra help so that she could get caught up. It has been two weeks and she is still not caught up."

Thinking about this situation, it dawned on me that the term *caught up* could have a negative connotation. What was going to happen to the employee when she got *caught up*? Would she be without anything to do? Would she be bored? And, besides, was it really possible to get caught up? Each new day brings with it both new and repetitious work and new and old projects. That means there is always something to do.

I realized I too had been frustrated for years trying to get caught up. As I repeated the term *caught up*, I felt a tightness in my abdomen, a feeling of being hurried. I had felt hurried for years. Suddenly I felt a shift in my energy level when I realized that the worker, my client, and I had been hindered by our negative sensory response to the term *caught up*. Since my client and I both had busy and productive businesses, we wouldn't ever get caught up. There would always be work to do. However, we could get *current* and stay current. With getting current as my new aim my body felt suddenly relaxed. Using a different term to express my goal created a very different feeling.

My client, her employee, and I have lessened our frustration and increased our satisfaction by switching our objective from getting *caught up* to staying *current*.

> *Whatever your hand finds to
> do, do it with your might . . .*
> *Ecclesiastes 9:10*

*It is only by risking our persons
from one hour to another that we
live at all.*

William James

Imagine yourself invited to a magnificent banquet. It is the most elaborate banquet you will ever have the opportunity to attend. You groom yourself well, and wear your finest clothes.

You arrive at the banquet hall. It is elaborately decorated, filled with magnificent arrangements of long-stemmed roses. You move from one arrangement to another to see how many varieties you recognize. As you examine a rose you prick yourself on a thorn. Quickly you lose interest in the roses and move toward the banquet table.

You have never seen so much food in your whole life. Since you are a connoisseur of fine food you are having a field day. You look at the first dish carefully and sample it sparingly to discern how it was prepared and what is in it. You check your analysis with someone who has just eaten and, sure enough, you were right. Feeling very pleased with yourself you move on to the next dish and repeat the process. You really do know as much about food as you thought!

The banquet is over and the guests are leaving. Now you realize that although you've had a great time nibbling and guessing the ingredients in each dish you have not eaten enough of anything to satisfy your hunger.

The banquet is life. Do you quickly turn away from the beauty if it gives you a little pain? Are you just studying it and analyzing it, or partaking of it and participating in it?

I am the bread of life.
John 6:48

GOALS

In the long run men hit only what they aim at.
Henry David Thoreau

To drift is to be in hell;
To be in heaven is to steer.
  George Bernard Shaw

You have just heard that you have won a trip. You can go anyplace you choose. All expenses are paid.

The first thing you have to do is decide if you want to go. If you do you will need to decide where. The next decision is how and when you will travel. Then you will have to make decisions about packing, pocket money, and immunizations.

Most folks don't take trips without choosing where they want to go, getting clear directions on how to get there, and arranging reliable transportation. Yet these same people may never consider choosing where they want to go in the far more important journey of life. On our journey through life we take many trips: these are our goals along the way. Our goals are what give us direction and keep us on the right road. Without them we don't know which road to take.

Have you noticed how many active people die soon after they retire? That may be because they didn't plan a new road to go down. With nowhere to go they deteriorate and even die. When some people don't have anyplace to go they simply stay in bed in the morning or move through their days aimlessly.

Having goals is fundamental to everything we do. Goals are essential to our mental and emotional well-being. What the goals are is not as important as the fact that they exist. Goals give our lives meaning and purpose and help us choose the roads we want to travel.

Life can happen to you or you can happen to life by setting your goals and committing yourself to achieving them.

> *. . . if therefore thine eye be*
> *single, thy whole body shall*
> *be full of light.*
> *Matthew 6:22 (KJV)*

To think we are able is almost to
be so; to determine an attainment is
frequently attainment itself. Earnest
resolution has often seemed to have
about it almost a savor of omnipotence.
                                    S. Smiles

The day was almost gone and I was feeling frustrated because I had not accomplished much. As I reflected on what had gone amiss, it occurred to me that I had not accomplished anything because I had begun the day with nothing particular in mind to accomplish. It became clear that lacking instruction from me as to what I wanted, my mind didn't know what to do.

I fantasized that without goals my mind was like a big jet plane all revved up with nowhere to go. Once the goal is established, the mind, like the jet plane, is ready and able to perform.

I had talked about writing this book for quite awhile and written a few essays from time to time. It wasn't until I gave myself a deadline to complete the book that I chose not to do other things that I enjoyed more than writing. Once I made the commitment, I had given a clear directive to my subconscious.

Writing and choosing an environment in which to write became a priority, not just something that I would do someday. Once the commitment was made and there weren't any conflicting goals, everything fell into place. I was able to take some time off and get away from distractions. The perfect cottage was offered for my stay. Typists became available to me. It all came together like magic.

Do you know what you really want from life? Commit yourself to achieving it; then your mind will know what to do.

Commit your work to the Lord
and your plans will be established.
Proverbs 16:3

108

Beware what you set your heart upon.
For it surely shall be yours.
Ralph Waldo Emerson

When Marsha took my class she had just finished a government-sponsored training program and was earning the minimum wage. Six months after completing the class she wrote a letter telling me how the goal-setting methods she had learned really worked.

"I was driving down the street and there, sitting on a used car lot, was my car," she wrote, "a black Thunderbird with red leather interior. I went in and told them that I had been visualizing myself driving that car for six months and that I wanted to try it out.

"The car is mine," she continued. "I got it all by myself, on my signature, without any help from anyone.

"Thank you for teaching me to write my goals down and visualize them each day," she concluded. "It really works."

As I read her letter I thought, "Thank you, Marsha, for not sharing your goal with me. I might have thought it my responsibility as your teacher to inquire if the goal was realistic on your salary." She was teaching me that what appeared unrealistic to me did not have to be unrealistic for someone else. With her goals to shoot for, Marsha didn't stay a minimum wage earner very long.

Eighteen months later I heard from her again. She had taken a course in real estate and moved back to her home city. She wanted me to know that the goal-setting methods were still working; she had quickly become top real-estate agent of the year.

Marsha has been a beautiful mirror for proving that regardless of the circumstances, once we determine what we want and are willing to be responsible for achieving it the mind goes to work to bring it about.

> *... now nothing will be restrained*
> *from them, which they have imagined*
> *to do.*
> *Genesis 11:6 (KJV)*

I have begun several times many things,
and I have often succeeded at last.
Benjamin Disraeli

We were in the process of doing some remodeling. The man we hired to do the painting was a most remarkable person. After his third day on the job I learned that he was seventy-six years old. In no way would I ever have suspected he was a day over sixty. I marveled as I watched him paint a twelve-foot ceiling. I watched in awe of his activity and agility. He smiled a mischievous little smile, and his eyes twinkled as he began to tell me how he had had cancer seven years before, and all about the treatment and complications he had undergone. He left the hospital in a wheelchair. The doctor told him and his wife that he would never walk again, and that he must resign himself to that fact. Still smiling, he said, "You know, I just accepted that as a challenge."

As he related his experience I understood that he had set out to rebuild his health. He didn't tell others, not even his wife, what he was going to do; he just did it. Before me was a living example of the power of determination. As I thought back through my life I realized that whenever I've had an inner determination to accomplish something, I have always succeeded. And when the determination was real, there wasn't any need to talk about it.

Thank you, sir, for the living mirror.

> *... and does not doubt in his heart,*
> *but believes that what he says will*
> *come to pass, it will be done for him.*
> *Mark 11:23b*

Be a lamp in the chamber if you
cannot be a light in the sky.
George Eliot

Years ago, when I was participating in a Transactional Analysis program, we were instructed to decide what we wanted said about us on our tombstone and to share it with the class the following week.

I kept thinking that it takes most people a good part of their lives to make that decision, and I only had a week. As I thought about it during the week I came to realize that the real question being asked was, "What do you want your life to be about?" Toward the end of the week I knew I wanted to have made some kind of difference when my life was over. So I decided I wanted my tombstone to read simply, "She made a difference."

I didn't have any grandiose ideas about doing anything majestic, or even anything specific. Making a difference simply became an intention, a purpose for my life. Keeping uppermost in my mind the desire to make a difference has opened the door to many very interesting experiences. It has also given me motivation to get out of bed in the morning. When I keep focused on making a difference, that intention affects all I do and the way I do it.

Do you want meaning and purpose in your life? Ask yourself, "What do I want said about me on my tombstone?"

To them who by patient continuance
in well doing seek for glory and
honor and immortality, eternal life . . .
Romans 2:7 (KJV)

111

The blossom cannot tell what becomes of its odor, and no man can tell what becomes of his influence.
                    Henry Ward Beecher

After I had decided that I wanted my life to be about making a difference, it took me several more years to realize that everyone did make a difference; in fact one could not *not* make a difference. The only choice we have is whether or not we make a *positive* difference.

The parent who neglects his child is making a difference in the child's life. The employee who does not show up at work when she is expected is making a difference in that business. When one person in a relationship will not communicate, that person is making a difference in the relationship. Yes, what we are and do influences and affects those around us. Knowing this we can consciously decide to make our influence positive.

I discovered that it is only when I am clear on my intention to make a positive difference that it is likely to happen. When I have the clear intent of making a positive difference, I stop and think before I speak; I ask myself if what I am about to say is really helpful or supportive. That makes a positive difference in the outcome of my communications.

This same intention in my work has increased my motivation and my effectiveness and given me a feeling of excitement. I find I'll redo any work that will get better results if done a different way, and I constantly look for ways to help my students integrate the concepts I teach. Wanting to make a positive difference has been one of the most motivating and energizing factors in my life.

Will you experiment with intending to make a positive difference and see how it affects your world?

So then, as we have opportunity, let us do good to all men . . .
                    Galatians 6:10

112

LOVE

Money is like love; it kills slowly and painfully the one who withholds it, and it enlivens the other who turns it upon his fellow man.

Kahlil Gibran

To love is to want to give and above
all give oneself. A perfect love is
the perfect gift of oneself without
thought of reward or return.

R. H. J. Stewart

Writers have been telling us for centuries that the secret of happiness is to love others. The Scriptures tell us over and over again to love one another.

Whenever I heard or read this idea I acknowledged agreement and played the role of a warm, loving human being. However, being honest with myself and getting in touch with the actual me, I realized I had spent most of my life trying to get other people to love me, not really concerned about loving them.

I had been doing things I really did not want to do, hoping to win love and approval. Communication was difficult because I frequently withheld the truth, not for fear of hurting others, as I had thought; rather, I was acting out of fear that I wouldn't be loved. I realized how crazy this was one day when I became aware that I was trying to win the love of someone I didn't even like.

Realizing I had spent at least the first half of my life seeking love from others and had not met with fulfillment, I decided I would spend the last half of my life giving love. I decided to experiment with the idea of giving love and expecting nothing in return. Right away I began to experience a feeling of joy and fulfillment. I really saw people I had not seen before. I became aware of how often I had been indifferent. An estranged relationship was healed without a word being said. I started communicating in an honest and direct way, and people listened. It was wonderful. Even though I'm not as loving as I want to be I feel as if a song is being sung silently within me.

Are you willing to experiment with giving love and expecting nothing back? A more loving world can start with you and me.

Make love your aim . . .
1 Corinthians 14:1

If you wish to be loved, love.
Seneca

William owns two very large and successful businesses. He sits on several boards, holds office in his professional organizations, and is a success by all the standards most of the world uses to judge success.

Yet William sat in my office terrified, almost immobilized. The company picnic was coming up and he was scared to attend. When I questioned him about his fears, he replied, "Well, at work people listen to me and respect me because I am the boss, but they really don't like me or care about me as a person." I asked him whether he cared about his employees as people.

"Oh yes," he responded. He listed all the fringe benefits he made available to his employees. They were really above-average benefits!

"As desirable as those benefits are, William, I wonder how you acknowledge their being. Do you make an effort to find out what is important to them or inquire about their personal interests?"

Shaking his head, he said, "No, I guess I don't."

"William, it sounds to me like you would like your employees to love you. Is that right?"

"You are right, that is exactly what I want," he replied. I assured him that I understood that need and had spent a lot of my energy seeking love too. One day it had dawned on me that I could never really experience love from another person. I could only experience the *form* that that love took. Sometimes the form was recognizable as love and sometimes it wasn't. If I really wanted to experience love I had to give it. My suggestion was that a sure way to experience love at the picnic was to give it.

He looked at me with the most amazed expression and said, "I've been looking under the wrong rock."

Are you looking for love under the wrong rock?

A new commandment I give to you,
love one another . . .
John 13:34

115

There is only one kind of love,
but it has a thousand guises.
La Rochefoucauld

A saddened woman sat across from me, her pretty face distorted with pain because she did not feel loved. I asked her what it would take for her to feel loved. She replied, "Hugging and touching." I asked her if she was hugged and touched as a child and she replied, "No, not at all. I know my parents loved me, but they were not demonstrative."

The next client to enter my office was a beautiful young woman with a brilliant mind and an enviable career. She was also in pain. She was feeling that she had never been loved and never would be. I asked her what it would take for her to feel loved. She responded, "For someone to keep check on me. To call to see if I made it where I am going, or to see what I am doing, or if I am alright." (I shuddered; the last thing I wanted was someone to keep check on me.) I asked her if that was what her parents had done when she was little. She said, "No, in fact they could have cared less where I was or what I was doing."

Such different concepts fascinated me and I began to ask other people what would make them feel loved. Each person had a different idea of what love was. If others did not fulfill that image, the person didn't feel loved. Most people's picture of love is either what they received as children or what they wanted as children and did not receive. What is your picture?

If you want an interesting insight into your relationships, start asking the people in your life what their concept of love is. What is it they need in order to feel loved? Was it what they got as children—or didn't get as children?

As the Father has loved me,
so have I loved you; abide
in my love.
John 15:9

116

GOD

Religion is the first thing and the last thing, and until man has found God, and been found by God, he begins at no beginning and works to no end.

H. G. Wells

Everyone who is seriously involved in the
pursuit of science becomes convinced that
a Spirit is manifest in the Laws of the
Universe—a Spirit vastly superior to that
of man, and one in the face of which we,
with our modest powers, must feel humble.

Albert Einstein

While reading the newspaper one day I became conscious of the television being on in the room. There was a science-fiction movie showing. It was about a man from another planet. The man was talking to a young boy who had a speech problem. The man said to the boy, "Ask the light in you to help you." Nothing happened. Again, he repeated, shouting, "Ask the light in you to help you."

I sat there transfixed as the young boy asked the light in him for help and got the help he needed. The scene struck a chord within me. I could imagine God saying, "You need only ask, I'm here."

Conceptually I knew the light was in us; in reality, I still looked for the light everywhere except within myself. I even talked to the light located at least seven planets removed. Seeing the movie moved the concept from my head to my gut; it became real.

Where are you looking for the light?

. . . He has given us light . . .
Psalms 118:27

All God's giants have been weak
men who did great things because
they reckoned on His being there.
                    J. Hudson Taylor

The idealist/perfectionist side of my personality and the actual me are often worlds apart. For years I kept myself feeling inferior or inadequate by demanding that I live up to my ideals. I became OK when I finally accepted the fact that I wasn't OK. I had flaws; I simply did not meet my standards.

I still have ideals. They motivate me. They give me goals to work toward. In the meantime, I'm OK as I am.

I was able to give up my unrealistic expectations by studying the lives of God's giants. Noah, whom God found worthy to spare from the flood, got drunk and lay naked when the flood was over. David, a man after God's own heart, killed a man in order to have the man's wife. Abraham, a man God chose to bless all the nations of the earth, lied about Sarah, his wife, to save his own life.

The list could go on. While God did not approve of these acts, there is evidence that He did not reject or abandon these men because of their misdeeds. He continued to accept them, and to bless them.

Observing God's continuing fellowship with these flawed men has enabled me to accept God's grace and mercy.

What then shall we say to this?
If God is for us, who is against
us?
Romans 8:31

God gives every bird food, but
He does not throw it into the
nest.

J. G. Holland

For years I was in conflict over the question of what part God plays in our lives. How much does God do and how much do we do? Sometimes I did nothing while trying to figure this enigma out.

After listening to many theories from different sources, I finally decided to look at Jesus as a role model. As I looked to see what God had done for Jesus, I didn't find any evidence that God had done anything *for* Him. There was much evidence that God did a lot *through* Him.

Jesus said, "By myself I can do nothing." (JBP) He made it clear that he got His power from His Father. Finally, the picture began to form for me. God did not do anything for Jesus; Jesus had to go through the process of doing. At the same time, God provided Him with the power and motivation. God needed Jesus to fulfill His mission; Jesus needed God to accomplish that mission. An interdependency existed.

When I am working with a person who has had a traumatic experience, I ask in prayer for the client to be given a new perspective, a different interpretation of the situation. I've witnessed some phenomenal experiences with immediate changes.

After I shared with a friend some of the results of these prayers, my friend looked at me and said, "Bobbi, you are the one who does that."

"You could be right," I said. "However, you should have seen the results when I was doing it all by myself." My friend grinned and acknowledged that he too had noticed a difference when he did not ask God's help and attempted things alone, and when he did ask God to assist him.

Letting go of me *or* Him, and becoming a me *and* Him—an *us*—has certainly made a difference in my life. All it takes is an invitation. He's waiting.

. . . and how tremendous is the power
available to us who believe in God.
That power is the same divine energy
which was demonstrated in Christ.
Ephesians 1:19

You can within yourself find a
mighty unexplored kingdom in which
you can dwell in peace if you will.
Russell H. Conwell

There are many people, I find, who base much of their lives on fantasy. One such fantasy that I frequently encounter is the idea that if we were *really* lovable, people would like us, accept us, and always be there when we need them. When that doesn't happen, we deduce that there must be *something* wrong with us.

Jesus, who was Love personified, did not win any popularity contests. In fact, His love led to His being killed. Many rejected Him then, and many still do. When He was in the garden going through His own inner struggle and facing death, He asked His disciples to stay awake and keep watch with Him. Instead they went to sleep. They went to sleep because of their human weakness, not because something was amiss in Jesus. He was perfect, yet He did not get His friends to stay awake and give Him moral support. One of His best friends denied even knowing Him.

Much of the time other people are unable to meet our needs because of their own human weaknesses. Recognizing that Jesus was abandoned in His hour of need has enabled me to give up my self-pity when my loved ones don't meet my needs. Seeing that despite His perfection He was not always liked or accepted has certainly released me from my fantasy of total or universal acceptance. I hope this thought can release you, too.

And when he rose from prayer,
he came to the disciples and
found them sleeping . . .
Luke 22:45

121

To be alone with Silence is
to be alone with God.
Samuel Miller Hageman

Magazines, newspapers, and television keep us well informed on the need to reduce stress in our lives. Emphasis is put on the need for some form of relaxation. Without some form of diversion from our normal activities we may suffer from burnout or disease.

Techniques for reducing stress abound. It is not more and better techniques that we need. What many people do need is permission in their own minds to do something that isn't "meaningful" or "productive." I too am grounded in the Puritan work ethic and I found it hard to learn to relax and do nothing.

It wasn't until I noticed how often Jesus withdrew to be alone that it occurred to me that if He needed time for Himself, you and I aren't likely to be any different. Jesus modeled what modern science is teaching. There was work to be done and Jesus withdrew. People were present to hear His teachings and sick people were there waiting to be healed, yet He withdrew. As long as we are participating in life—until the day that we die—there will be work to be done. In the meantime, like Jesus, at times we need to be alone.

What works best for me and keeps me running smoothly is one hour by myself each morning. This allows me to contact the indwelling spirit. Doing nothing is doing something. It is "re-creation" time. Do you find that you need to be alone at times? Do you take it?

Be still, and know that
I am God . . .
Psalms 46:10

To err is human, to forgive divine.
Alexander Pope

Close your eyes and envision the following scene: You are with a mob of people at Golgotha and are standing near three men hanging on crosses. You and the people are directing most of your attention to the man in the center: Jesus. You are mocking and jeering at Him. You say, "You are the Son of God, save yourself."

Jesus raises his head toward the heavens and says, "Father, forgive them for they know not what they do."

From among the mass of people you shout back, "What do you mean, we don't know what we are doing? We know exactly what we are doing. We are crucifying you. It is you who don't know what you are doing."

Jesus' eyes fall on the people below Him. Looking straight at them He says, "No, Father, these people are innocent. They think they know what they are doing, and they do not. Forgive them."

For about two weeks this scene dominated my consciousness. It affected me in a profound way. As I began to look at my life, I remembered times I was sure I knew what I was doing only to find out later that I hadn't really known. I knew that I had been responsible for all that I had done. Then I began to wonder, could I be responsible and innocent—that is, not guilty—at the same time? Was forgiveness the experience of seeing or accepting responsibility without affixing blame?

For the first time I could think about a person who had committed a grave injustice against me and forgive him. Even though he had thought he knew what he was doing, he had not. He was innocent. And my pain was suddenly gone.

Seeing myself and others as sometimes not knowing what we are doing has given me compassion and the ability to forgive. Can it help you, too?

It is through Him, at the cost
of His own blood, that we are
redeemed, freely forgiven through
that free and generous Grace which
has overflowed into our lives and
given us wisdom and insight.
Ephesians 1:7–8 (JBP)

123

*The master spirit of the earth
shall not sleep peacefully upon
the wind till the needs of the
least of you are satisfied.*
                    Kahlil Gibran

As Cherie and I were watching the rain fall she told me that recently she had been angry with God. She related that she had said to God, "OK, if You are real and loving, why are You so unfair? Why do You give some people so much and some people so little?"

With these questions on her mind, she went for a walk in the rain. As she walked she noticed a collection of containers that had been put out to catch rainwater. Some had very narrow openings and some had very wide openings. The containers with large openings caught more rainwater; the smaller the opening the less rainwater the container caught.

This made Cherie realize that God was willing to give to all. Some people are not open to receive very much from Him, while others are very open and receive a lot. Cherie chuckled as she pictured herself as having a long narrow neck with a stopper in it. How large is your opening?

*"Fear not, little flock, for it
is your Father's good pleasure
to give you the kingdom."*
                    Luke 12:32

I myself believe that the evidence
for God lies primarily in inner
personal experiences.
William James

As I was pondering what it could mean to be the child of God, my thoughts turned to what it means to me to be a parent.

When my sons were small and stubbed their toes, I was there to give them comfort. When they soiled their pants I was there to clean them up. When they had an important lesson to learn, I was willing to let them learn the hard way when necessary. When there was real danger, I was there to protect them. When they were troubled, I was there to listen, even though sometimes they weren't ready to talk. I was there to offer guidance and counsel, although often they didn't seek it.

I don't approve of all they do, and I still love them. In fact there is nothing they can do that would keep me from loving them. There are things they can do that would cause me pain. There is nothing they can do that would cause me to disown them. These are some of the strengths of the love I have for my children. Yet even my finite mind recognizes that God's love for His children must be far, far greater than this.

Perhaps He sees us as we see our children: learning, making mistakes. What appear to us as gross errors may appear to Him as soiled pants.

This analogy helped me to get our relationship with God in perspective and to know that He accepts us, dirty pants and all.

In Him we live and move and have
our being . . .
Acts 17:28

125

The most important thing in the world is not
to know the Lord's will but to know the Lord.
                                    Wallace Bays

I've been a religious person most of my life, and I've always attended church on a regular basis and learned a lot about God. Learning about God was interesting, and it did give me some guideposts to live by. Still, there was something missing.

When I set out to discover what it was that was missing, I got a picture of what I was doing. It was like reading everything I could about the president of the United States. I could be with other people who wanted to know about the president. We could all get together and talk about him. No matter how interested we were, or how much we knew about him, something would be missing until we met the president and talked with him personally. We could know a lot about him and still not know him.

Once I had determined that this was the way it must work with God, too, I decided to find out if God could be experienced.

If we want to know a person we have to let that person know it. We have to be available to him. We have to spend time with him. Also we have to listen to him. With the desire to know God, I created an inner room in my mind and told God I wanted to meet Him there. Words aren't adequate to explain what happened. All I can say is that I could and do experience an energy that I acknowledge as God. The difference between knowing about and knowing is like the difference between operating for years on 110 volts, then suddenly discovering you have 220 volts available. My missing part wasn't missing anymore. I felt complete. Slowly I began to notice changes in my attitudes and the way I dealt with people.

Have you experienced the difference between knowing about God and knowing God?

"If a man loves me, he will
keep my word, and my Father
will love him, and we will
come to him and make our
home with him."
John 14:23

126

EPILOGUE

A bad book is as much a labor to write as a good one, it comes as sincerely from the author's soul.

Aldous Huxley

As I finish this book I see many things more clearly. I am more conscious than ever of how much we all need one another. Many people have touched me personally. I am grateful to each of them for allowing me to experience myself and for affirming that I am.

I have always been able to relate to the old commercial, "Please, Mother, I'd rather do it myself." Doing things alone and on my own has been a strong drive in my life. Rereading this book gave me a vivid picture of how very little I've done alone. That awareness made me feel very small and insignificant—a very humbling experience.

Yet as I saw our connectedness to each other and to the Divine Source, I also felt larger than life, and very powerful. I sensed my smallness and my bigness simultaneously—really experiencing our interdependency.

I share our stories with the hope that we can be your mirrors—to reflect your own light. As you read these vignettes I hope you too will allow yourself to be touched and affirmed.

I have always loved you.
Malachi 1:2 (TEV)

ALSO AVAILABLE

Sixteen hours of *Total Effectiveness Training*, a complete program in twelve cassettes in which Bobbi Sims covers many of the topics discussed in *Making a Difference in Your World*. Available at a special price to readers of this volume.

For further information on these cassettes, as well as on the author's seminars, lectures, and workshops, write:

Bobbi Sims
3454 Santa Fe
Corpus Christi, Texas 78411